Living Off-Grid
Homesteading 101

- Buy Your Land & Build Your Dream House
- Build Solar or Alternative Energy Systems
- Collect & Purify Rainwater
- Sustainable Year-Round Gardening
- Master Food Storage Techniques
- Expand Your Pantry by Raising Chickens
- Learn Homesteader Security & Community

Living Off-Grid: Homesteading 101

LIVING OFF-GRID, HOMESTEADING 101

Buy Your Land & Build Your Dream House, Build Solar or Alternative Energy Systems, Collect & Purify Rainwater, Sustainable Year-Round Gardening, Master Food Storage Techniques, Expand Your Pantry by Raising Chickens, Learn Homesteader Security & Community

© 2024, Viking Publications of Tennessee. All rights reserved.

Published by Viking Publications of Tennessee, 463 East Parkway, Gatlinburg TN 37738

No part of this publication may be reproduced, distributed, or transmitted in any form or by any means, including photocopying, recording, or other electronic or mechanical methods, without the prior written permission of the publisher, except in the case of brief quotations embodied in critical reviews and certain other noncommercial uses permitted by copyright law.

This book is a work of non-fiction. Any resemblance to actual events, locales, or persons, living or dead, is entirely coincidental.

Cataloging-in-Publication Data for this book is available from the Library of Congress.

ISBN: 9798883674487

Printed in the United States. First Edition: March 2024

Cover Design by Viking Publications of Tennessee

Interior Design by Viking Publications of Tennessee

For information regarding special discounts for bulk purchases, please contact Viking Publications of Tennessee, Facebook page: https://www.facebook.com/vikingpublicationsoftennessee.

LIMIT OF LIABILITY/DISCLAIMER OF WARRANTY: The publisher and the author make no representations or warranties with respect to the accuracy or completeness of the contents of this work and specifically disclaim all warranties, including without limitation warranties of fitness for a particular purpose. No warranty may be created or extended by sales or promotional materials. The advice and strategies contained herein may not be suitable for every situation. This work is sold with the understanding that the publisher is not engaged in rendering legal, accounting, or other professional services. If professional assistance is required, the services of a competent professional person should be sought. Neither the publisher nor the author shall be liable for damages arising herefrom. The fact that an organization or website is referred to in this work as a citation and/or a potential source of further information does not mean that the author or the publisher endorses the information the organization or website may provide or recommendations it may make.

Dedication

This book is dedicated to the Earth, our nurturing mother, and to all who dare to dream of a life more in sync with her rhythms, this book is dedicated to you.

Embarking on the journey of homesteading is not merely a lifestyle choice but a profound act of reconnection with the natural world. It is a path less traveled, where the fruits of labor taste sweeter because they come from the soil you've toiled and the systems you've crafted with your own hands. This book is a beacon for those who yearn to step off the beaten path and forge a life of self-reliance, sustainability, and harmony with nature.

To the pioneers of the past, whose wisdom and resilience have paved the way for us, we owe a debt of gratitude. Their lives, rooted in the principles of homesteading, remind us of the strength and fortitude inherent in living closely with the land. Inspired by their example, this book aims to bridge the gap between traditional knowledge and modern innovation, guiding you through the process of building your dream homestead from the ground up.

In these pages, you will find a comprehensive guide to buying and transforming land into a sanctuary that reflects your values and vision. From constructing your dream house with attention to ecological impact, to installing solar panels or other alternative energy systems, every step is a stride towards sustainability.

Water, the lifeblood of the homestead, is revered and conserved here. You will learn to collect and purify rainwater, ensuring that every drop is used with respect and gratitude. The cycle of life continues in the garden, where sustainable practices allow you to grow food year-round, reducing your footprint and nourishing your body and soul.

Food storage is an art and a science, a means of preserving the bounty of the land. This book delves into techniques that have stood the test of time, ensuring that you can enjoy the fruits of your labor, even in the leaner months. Raising chickens expands your pantry and connects you to the cycle of life on your homestead, each egg a symbol of self-sufficiency.

Lastly, the homesteader's security and sense of community are paramount. This book explores how to create a safe, supportive environment, fostering connections with fellow homesteaders and the land itself.

To all who embark on this journey, may you find joy in every sunrise and solace in every sunset. Welcome to the world of homesteading, where every day is an opportunity to live more fully in harmony with the Earth.

Viking Publications of Tennessee

Living Off-Grid: Homesteading 101

Table Of Contents

Introduction 10

Chapter 1

Acquiring Land for Your Homestead 13

Navigating the Real Estate Market 13
Key Factors to Consider when Choosing Land 17
Understanding Zoning and Land Use Regulations 19
Investing Wisely: Financial Considerations................... 22

Chapter 2

Designing and Building a Sustainable Home 27

Overview of Eco-Friendly Home Design 27
Planning Your Sustainable Home 29
Energy Efficiency in Home Construction...................... 32
Balancing Comfort and Sustainability 34
What Size House is Comfortable?............................ 35

Chapter 3

Solar Power Simplified 39

The Basics of Solar Power................................... 39
Installation and Maintenance of Solar Panel Systems 42
Cost Benefit Analysis of Solar Energy......................... 44
Troubleshooting Common Solar Power Issues................. 46

Chapter 4
Exploring Alternative Energy Sources 51

Wind Power Basics 51
Hydroelectric Power for Homesteaders 53
Potential of Biomass Energy 56
Picking Your Power Source................................... 58

Chapter 5
Rainwater Collection and Storage 63

Building an Efficient Rainwater Harvesting System 63
Storage Solutions for Rainwater 65
Ensuring Water Quality 67
Legal Aspects of Rainwater Collection 69

Chapter 6
Navigating Water Purification 75

Health Risks of Contaminated Water 75
DIY Water Purification Methods.............................. 78
Purchasing and Maintaining Water Purifiers 80
Water Purification in Emergency Situations 82

Chapter 7
Year-Round Food Production 87

Your Homestead Garden...................................... 87
Planning Your Homestead Garden 87
Climate Specific Farming Techniques......................... 93
Extending the Growing Season 95
Pest Control and Organic Farming Methods.................. 97

Chapter 8

Preserving the Harvest: Canning and Storing Your Produce 103

Home Canning Basics 103
Dehydrating Fruits and Vegetables 106
Root Cellaring Techniques 108
Safe Food Storage Practices 110

Chapter 9

Raising and Harvesting Chickens for the Homestead 113

Introduction 113
Which Breed of Chicken is Best for Your Homestead? 113
Chickens' Quirky Behavior: 115
Setting Up Your Coop 116
Daily Care & Management: 118
Keeping Your Flock Healthy 119
Egg Production 120
Raising Chickens for Meat 121

Chapter 10

Ensuring Your Homestead's Security 127

Evaluating Your Homestead's Vulnerabilities 127
Basic Security Measures for Every Homesteader 129
Advanced Security Systems for the Homestead 130
Emergency Preparedness 132

Chapter 11

The Homesteader's Community - Weaving the Social Fabric of Self-Sufficiency 137

The Importance of Community for Homesteaders. 138
Networking with Nearby Homesteaders 139
Engaging with the Wider Community 141
Handling Opposition and Skepticism. 143

Conclusion. 148

Living Off-Grid: Homesteading 101

Introduction

The "gentleman farmer" of the past is a portrait from yesteryear for today's modern homesteader, envisioning a self-assured, self-sufficient, country lifestyle, rejecting today's fast-paced lifestyle! You are not alone in feeling that tug - that pull, toward a life less muddied with the demands of current society. In this fast-paced, digital world, more and more of us yearn for something less complicated, something that roots us to the earth, and gives us a desire to control our own destiny. That is where the need for self-sufficiency comes in, and it's a need you feel right down to your toes.

Let's talk about the journey you will experience in this book. One of the first questions I was asked while talking about writing this book was "What is the difference between a "homesteader" and a "prepper"? It seemed to me that there is an undercurrent, a nervousness people have regarding the future. History shows us there will always be changes in employment, government, economics – as a matter of fact, we just suffered through a global pandemic! Yes, there is a lot of uncertainty in this life. So, to answer the question, I think it is the different path that calls to those who want to step up their "security" game; to be ready for anything life throws their way and have the capability to defend themselves. Preppers embrace numerous practical, reliable security measures however, seem a bit more apocalyptic, as seen in the popular television shows such as "Doomsday Preppers".

Homesteaders are mindful but seem to be less concerned about World War III or another Civil War, well-aware of their security needs, they are more focused on enjoying their life off the land, caring for their families using environmentally balanced practices. Everyone living off-grid needs to consider they are living in a remote area and need to be prepared for a natural disaster. And let's face it, with the way things are going these days, who can afford not to be prepared? But this isn't just about being ready for the tough times—it's more about building a life that's sustainable, filled with work, joyfully supporting your family and your property, all in tune with the rhythms of nature.

Picture an eco-friendly, successful, self-sufficient lifestyle. This is the vision we're working towards together. It's a life where your home is a haven, powered by the sun or other forms of alternative energy. Where rainwater is captured and put to good use, and where the food on your table is grown in

Introduction

your own backyard—year-round. It's about building something that lasts and something that nurtures not just our bodies, but also our souls. We are all yearning for peace of mind and satisfaction.

In the pages that follow, we'll dive into the nuts and bolts of land acquisition, sustainable home construction, and the ins and outs of solar and alternative energy sources. We'll explore the necessary methods of rainwater collection and how to prepare and store clean, hygienic water for human consumption. We will get our hands dirty, learning how to grow produce that can sustain your family which is absolutely magical as you nurture seed to produce on the dinner table. We will discuss soil science, what crops to grow, companion planting, and ultimately how to extend the growing season thereby feeding you and your family 365 days a year. We will also cover the how's and why's of successfully storing your harvest to ensure that no matter what, you and your loved ones will be well-fed.

But who am I to guide you through all this? Well, I've been where you are. With degrees in biology and engineering tucked under my belt, I have experienced buying and selling land, designing, remodeling and building homes. I've installed solar panel systems, retention lagoons either with my own two hands or by working with outside contractors. My concern for our planet's future and the impacts of global warming have always driven me to take action—and now, I'm here to share that journey with you.

So, if you're ready to roll up your sleeves and get your hands dirty (literally!), let's get started. We've got a lot of ground to cover, and I can't wait to walk you through every step of the way.

Welcome to your new adventure! Let's excel at this!

Living Off-Grid: Homesteading 101

Chapter 1

Acquiring Land for Your Homestead

There's an indescribable feeling that comes with staking your claim on a piece of the Earth that is uniquely yours. It's scary, intimidating and exhilarating. It's the first step in creating a space that echoes your values of sustainability and self-reliance. Securing that slice of paradise, that patch of potential, is both thrilling and daunting. It's not merely a transaction—it's a declaration of your commitment to yourself and your family. Let's face it, as far as we know, this life is our ultimate gift and perhaps our only chance at this lifetime, so let's make it count!!

The real estate market is a mass of unpredictable facts dependent on the fundamental analysis of economic indicators, interest rates, and consumer sentiment. TV pundits pontificate on GDP, Fed Rates and Unemployment Reports. Deciphering this tapestry is important to making informed decisions. However, it's important to realize that the goal is not to sell the high or buy the low, but to be close. Whether you're looking at sprawling acres or a modest plot, the principles of smart buying remain constant.

Navigating the Real Estate Market

The real estate market ebbs and flows, influenced by projected property value, both on a global and local scale. A well-informed buyer understands these movements are constantly in action. Knowledge of market trends helps in anticipating the best times to buy. For instance, an uptick in interest rates may cool down a previously hot market, providing a perfect opportunity to buy land at a more reasonable price. Conversely, an economic boom could see land values skyrocket, making it crucial to sell property and act swiftly. Market timing is more of an artform than a science and is something to be aware of, however, again, remember it is unlikely to sell the top and buy the bottom.

Evaluating property listings goes beyond the aesthetics of rolling hills or wooded areas. It demands a keen eye for what the land holds beneath its beauty. Soil quality, access to water, access to the internet and cell phone reception and the potential for other nearby real estate developments are just as critical as the view. Learning to read property listings for these details is like learning a new language. It's about understanding terms like 'percolation test' for septic systems, 'easements' that may affect land use, and 'setbacks' that dictate building proximity to the property lines. Before purchasing any land you should know these numbers. How many bedrooms does the property "perc" for? What are the distances for the easements and setbacks for each property line. These all factor into the question "What is a sound investment"?

When it comes to negotiating the purchase price, remember it's not just about how much you can afford—it's also about the land's true worth and future value. You need good soil and the "lay of the land" needs to withstand sudden weather changes, rainstorms and runoff water. This is where due diligence pays off. Before making an offer, gather as much information as possible about the land. Get a copy of the survey, look into the sale history, current use, and any future developments planned in the area, as these can all affect the land's value.

Consider consulting an experienced real estate agent to help sift through what is currently available on the market, and what may become available in the future. Chances are you will need to use the services of a real estate agent eventually, so why not get them to work early? Provide the agent with a list of parameters that are important to you. This will help speed up the discovery process for your little piece of heaven.

Understanding Market Trends

Keeping a pulse on real estate market trends provides a strategic advantage. It's like predicting the weather patterns before setting sail — it ensures a smoother journey. Use resources like the Federal Housing Finance Agency's House Price Index (HPI) to track historical price trends. Local real estate agents can also offer insights into seasonal market fluctuations and long-term investment potential.

The trick lies in timing. Spring often ushers in a surge of listings as properties, quite literally, show in their best light. The end of summer may reveal motivated sellers looking to close deals before winter. And after a harsh winter, prices might soften, reflecting the hardships of the season.

Evaluating Property Listings

While evaluating property listings, your approach should be systematic. Start with the location and the land's topography and natural resources. Access to water, a clear view of the sun, and perhaps protection from prevailing winds are a factor. Are there slopes that could complicate construction or natural water sources that could be assets or deterrents?

Consider the property's potential for growth. Does it have enough space for your future plans; how about a greenhouse, a root cellar that can serve as a tornado shelter, if need be, or a workshop, or solar panel arrays? And don't forget to factor in the less tangible elements — does the land speak to your aesthetic and emotional desires?

Consider a visit to the local city and/or county planning department. This can be illuminating. You'll gain access to critical information on zoning laws, planned developments, or any environmental protections in place—factors that all play into the land's suitability for your homesteading dreams.

Proximity to Resources

While evaluating property listings, you also need to answer some basic personal questions such as: What does living off-grid mean to you? How remote do you want to be? What must you have and what can you do without? Is the property within a reasonable distance from your "necessary amenities" such as grocery stores, hospitals, and schools? Will your cellphone company provide adequate phone reception and an internet hot-spot? Will your internet access be provided via satellite? Are you comfortable with the distance to the nearest town or city for essentials that can't be produced on-site?

While the goal of homesteading is often to reduce reliance on external resources, no homestead is an island. Consider the proximity to support resources such as feed stores, hardware suppliers, as well as local farmers' markets, homesteading groups, or cooperative extensions where you can learn and share knowledge? These homesteader communities and networking can be invaluable, offering support, expertise, and camaraderie as you grow your homestead.

Negotiating Purchase Price

Negotiating the purchase price is perhaps where your homework pays the highest dividends. Arm yourself with as much information as possible. If the land has been on the market for a while, the seller may be more incentivized to negotiate, possibly accept a land contract or a lower offer. Comparable sales, often referred to as "comps," provide a benchmark; these are the recent sale prices of similar properties in the area. They will act as a guideline during conversations about pricing.

Approach the negotiation with respect and transparency, ready to present your case backed by facts. A well-articulated rationale for your offer price sets a professional tone for the negotiation. Speak with your bank prior to negotiating a land purchase to determine how much of a personal investment the bank will expect if you will be financing the land purchase. Typically financing a land purchase requires a 50% downpayment. Should the seller make a counteroffer that is unacceptable, don't be afraid to walk away especially if it stretches beyond your budget or the land's assessed value.

During these discussions, flexibility can be your ally. Sometimes, the terms of the sale—such as the closing date or contingencies—can be just as negotiable as the price. Quick closings and cash offers are a beneficial feature associated with any offer. Flexibility on these points might make the seller more amenable to adjusting the price in your favor.

Remember, the goal is to negotiate fair deal that reflects both the land's value and your investment in a sustainable future. It's a dance of give-and-take, where the final handshake seals a promise—a promise of a new beginning on a piece of land that will nurture not only your family's needs but also the planet's health. With the right approach, this initial step of land acquisition sets the stage for a homesteading venture where respect for nature and self-sufficiency go hand-in-hand.

Acquiring Land for Your Homestead

Key Factors to Consider when Choosing Land

Selecting the right piece of land for your homestead is a decision that resonates through every aspect of your future sustainability efforts. Each plot of earth presents its unique characteristics, and understanding these traits is crucial to aligning your homesteading dreams with reality. From the richness of the soil to the patterns of the sun's journey across the sky, the topography, water sources; every detail matters in creating a living space that is both sustainable and nurturing.

Due diligence is key when deciding whether this land is feasible for your homestead. Consider any legal encumbrances and easements regarding neighboring properties. How was the land used historically? Was it ever used for industrial use that could have left contamination or hazardous waste? Any evidence of Illegal dumping. Are there any endangered species or protected habitants, or conservation easements that restrict development and usage. Satisfactory answers to these questions is required.

Soil Quality

Soil is the foundation of any homestead. Its health dictates the vitality of your garden, the growth of your garden, orchard, and the sustainability of your land. Before deciding on a property, it's recommended to have the soil tested by your local USDA Extension Office, county Farm Service Agency, local Co-operative, or nearby university agricultural department.

To understand the soil's texture and structure you need to answer a few questions. Is it sandy and well-draining, or is it rich in clay, holding moisture and nutrients? Loamy soil, often considered ideal for farming, offers a balanced mix of sand, silt, and clay. It retains moisture and nutrients without becoming waterlogged. If the soil is less than ideal, don't despair. Composting, cover cropping, and green manures can improve soil health over time, turning even the most challenging dirt into fertile ground for your homestead. However, you need to know what you are buying and what sort of improvements may need to be made. This way you have an estimate as to the amount of time and money you need to improve the soil prior to purchasing.

A comprehensive soil analysis reveals nutrient levels, pH balance, and the presence of any contaminants that could affect your crops. Soil testing laboratories are typically available at state universities. For information about having a soil test performed, contact your local farm cooperative or your USDA Extension Service available in each county. These results will indicate whether you will need to amend the soil, which transcends into time and money.

Water Accessibility

Water is life, and ensuring your homestead has a reliable water source is imperative. Assess the property for existing water features such as streams, ponds, or springs. These can be invaluable for the viability of the homestead.

But it's not just about what's on the surface. Understanding the water table's depth and the availability of groundwater is essential if you plan to dig a well. Consider the annual rainfall in the area and whether it will meet your needs. If it falls short, look into the potential for rainwater harvesting and storage systems to bridge the gap.

Sunlight Exposure

Your homestead's solar exposure directly impacts your ability to grow food, harness solar energy, and even heat your home. Observe the property at different seasons and the time of day to understand the sun's path. Note any natural or man-made features that cast shade, particularly during the growing season. The Permaculture Research Institute features an article on charting the sun's motion in relation to your home at www.permaculturenews.org.

Ideally, your main garden and solar panels should have clear, unobscured view of the south–southwestern skies to maximize growth and energy production. Typically, the ideal tilt angle for solar panels should be the same as the latitude of the property. If you're in the northern hemisphere, remember that the sun will be lower in the sky during winter months, leading to less shaded areas during the winter. However, during the summer, if trees are located too close to the solar panels, they may block the sun and reduce energy production during the summer when the trees have their leaves out.

Local Climate

Climate plays a pivotal role in your homestead's potential. It influences what you can grow, the structures you build, and the energy systems you implement. Research the local climate, noting the average temperatures, precipitation patterns, and extreme weather risks such as droughts, floods, or hurricanes.

Acquiring Land for Your Homestead

This knowledge informs your decisions—from choosing the right crops for your garden to designing your home with natural climate control in mind. If you're in a region with harsh winters, consider how you'll manage snow removal and access to your property. In areas prone to heatwaves, look at the land's natural cooling features, such as shade trees or breezes.

Each of these factors—soil quality, water accessibility, sunlight exposure, and local climate—carries weight in your decision-making process. They shape not just the feasibility of your homesteading endeavors but also the quality of life you'll cultivate on your land. With careful consideration and planning, you can select a property that not only meets your needs but also thrives under your stewardship.

Understanding Zoning and Land Use Regulations

Securing land for your homestead is a pivotal first step, but it's just the beginning. What you can and cannot do on your newly acquired land hinges on a web of zoning laws and land use regulations. These rules, often established and enforced by local governments, are in place to ensure that land is used in a way that benefits the community and is in line with development plans. Violators of these codes may be subject to fines, lawsuits and even demolition of what was built improperly or without access. Like Ben Franklin said, "An ounce of prevention is worth a pound of cure."

Residential Zoning Laws

When exploring potential properties, it's crucial to be aware of the zoning classifications. But first, you need to know what you want to do on your property. Then, you will be able to determine if your property will allow you to do what you want.

Residential zones are primarily designated for residential homes and may have restrictions on the type of agricultural activities allowed. In some cases, there might be limitations on the number of animals you can keep or the size of structures you can build, or if you can build a dock on a body of water, etc.

It's wise to review the local zoning ordinance or speak with a representative from the local zoning office to get the specifics. The state Department of Natural Resources or Interior may also be of value. They can provide insights into what activities are permissible and which might require special permits or variances. For example, adding a wind turbine to your property may be subject to height restrictions or require approval from a board.

Agricultural Restrictions

In contrast, land zoned for agriculture often comes with more freedom for farming activities but might have its own set of guidelines to follow. These can include rules about the types of crops you can plant, the use of pesticides and fertilizers, or the management of water runoff. Some agricultural zones encourage preservation of the land for farming and may offer tax incentives or easements to do so.

Before you commit to a property, take the time to understand the agricultural policies that apply. Your real estate agent, county agricultural board, local university and State Department of Interior are good resources. This will prevent future hiccups when you're knee-deep in developing your homestead. If your plans include selling produce or other goods, you may also need to comply with regulations concerning commercial activities on agricultural land.

Building Codes

Building codes are another layer of regulation that can impact your homestead's development and the agencies enforcing these codes are typically city and county planning departments. These codes set forth the standards for construction to ensure safety and habitability. Be aware that permits typically require inspections by the governing body to ensure compliance. They cover a range of elements from building structural integrity to electrical and plumbing systems, and even energy efficiency.

As you plan your sustainable home or outbuildings, familiarize yourself with the building codes that will apply. This may influence your choice of building materials or techniques. For instance, if you're considering a straw bale home, you'll need to ensure that it meets the insulation and fire safety standards required by your local codes. In some regions, alternative building methods are welcomed and encouraged, while in others, they might be met with resistance.

The process of obtaining building permits is also dictated by these codes. Permits are a way for local authorities to review your plans and ensure they align with established standards. While this can sometimes be seen as a hurdle, it's also a safeguard—a way to ensure that the investment you're making in your homestead is sound and secure for yourself and the community.

Environmental Regulations

Environmental regulations are in place to protect the natural resources and ecosystems that surround us. These can range from restrictions on clearing land to rules governing the handling of wastewater. If your property includes wetlands or is home to endangered species, there may be additional government agencies you may need to consult with such as the Environmental Protection Agency (EPA) and Department of the Interior.

For example, if you're planning to draw water from a natural source or construct a pond, you may need to adhere to regulations regarding water rights and usage. Similarly, if you intend to install a septic system, it must comply with health department regulations that safeguard groundwater quality.

Understanding these regulations before you begin can save you from costly mistakes or delays. When in doubt, a consultation with USDA, Department of Natural Resources or with local conservation officials can offer advice and guidance.

Navigating these regulations may seem like a daunting task, but it's an unavoidable aspect of laying the groundwork for your homestead. Think of it as building a relationship with the land that respects the broader community and the environment. This foundation of knowledge ensures that as you build, grow, and nurture your homestead, you do so within a framework that supports your goals and safeguards the integrity of the landscape you've come to call home.

In the end, these zoning and land use regulations act as a guide, helping to shape the choices you make for your homestead. They prompt you to consider not only your vision but also the collective vision of the community and the ecological footprint you leave behind. With a clear understanding of these rules, you can proceed with confidence, knowing that your homesteading endeavors are not only sustainable and self-sufficient but also in harmony with the world around you.

Investing Wisely: Financial Considerations

Investing in land is as much a financial decision as it is an emotional one. It's the canvas on which you'll paint your future, but to make sure the picture is as beautiful as you envision, the numbers need to add up. A budget isn't just a spreadsheet with numbers; it's a reflection of your priorities and a roadmap to achieving your homestead dreams without financial strain.

Budgeting for Land Purchase

A well-thought-out budget acts as a compass, guiding you through the sea of financial decisions you'll face. It starts with a clear-eyed look at your finances – how much you have, how much you're willing to spend, and how much you'll need to keep aside for the multitude of other expenses that can crop up when establishing a homestead. (Pun intended 😆)

Breaking down the costs associated with acquiring land goes beyond the sticker price. There are property taxes, closing costs, commissions, and possibly the need for land surveys and environmental assessments. Your real estate agent, and banker are good sources for this information. Allocate funds for these additional expenses upfront to avoid surprises later on. It's prudent to consider the cost of developing the land post-purchase. Will you need to clear trees, install fencing, amend soil or bring in utilities? These can all add significant costs to your initial budget.

Crafting this budget calls for a balance between your current financial situation and your future goals. It might mean adjusting expectations or timelines, but it keeps your financial health front and center, ensuring that your homestead is built on solid ground.

Financing Options

Securing financing for land can be a different ballgame from a traditional home mortgage. Many lenders view land as a riskier investment, particularly if there's no residence already in place. This often translates to higher down payments and interest rates. That's why exploring all your financing options is a step you can't afford to skip.

Conventional loans are a go-to for many, but they're not the only game in town. Owner financing can be a viable alternative, where the seller acts as the lender, often with more flexible terms. In agricultural areas, you might find lenders who specialize in land and farming operations. These institutions understand the unique nature of land purchases and may offer more tailored loan products.

There are also government programs designed to support the purchase of land for agricultural purposes. For instance, the USDA offers loans targeted at new farmers, with attractive terms like lower down payments and subsidized interest rates. These programs can be competitive, but they're worth investigating if they align with your plans.

Regardless of the route you choose, ensure you understand the terms of your financing thoroughly. An attractive interest rate might be offset by a balloon payment down the road, or there could be penalties for early repayment. A clear understanding of these details prevents unexpected financial obstacles as you develop your homestead.

Long-term Value

When contemplating the investment in your homestead, it's essential to consider the long-term value of the land. This isn't just about potential resale value, though that's certainly part of the equation. It's also about the value that accrues from establishing a sustainable and self-sufficient lifestyle.

Improvements you make to the land, whether it's building a home, cultivating a garden, or installing renewable energy systems, can all increase the property's value. But more than that, they increase your self-reliance and resilience. This is value that doesn't show up in a bank statement but is felt in reduced living expenses and an enriched quality of life. Down the road, should you want to sell your homestead, for tax purposes you will need receipts for all the improvements to offset potential capital gains taxes.

Consider the potential for the land to generate income, which can provide financial stability and help offset costs. This might come from selling produce, offering agritourism experiences, or leasing part of the land for grazing. Investing in your homestead isn't just about spending money; it's about creating an asset that sustains itself and contributes to your financial well-being.

The investment in land is a long-term play, and the true value often unfolds over years or even generations. As the land yields its fruits and you adapt and grow with it, the initial financial outlay can turn into an investment that keeps on giving. This is the beauty of homesteading – It's not just a place to live; it's a living legacy.

As you weave your way through the financial tapestry of land acquisition, remember that each decision, each number, is a thread contributing to the overall strength and beauty of your homestead. With a solid financial plan in place, you position yourself to reap the rewards of a life built on sustainability, self-sufficiency, and harmony with the land.

References:

1) **4 Key Factors That Drive the Real Estate Market** - https://www.investopedia.com/articles/mortages-real-estate/11/factors-affecting-real-estate-market.asp

2) **9 Things to Know Before Buying Land for a Homestead** - https://www.theseasonalhomestead.com/9-things-to-know-before-buying-land-for-a-homestead/

3) **Consider Zoning Laws when Purchasing Homestead Land** - https://www.motherearthnews.com/sustainable-living/green-homes/consider-zoning-laws-purchasing-homestead-land-zbcz1907/

4) **Land Loans: Everything You Need to Know – The process of obtaining a land loan is trickier than obtaining a mortgage** - https://www.investopedia.com/articles/credit-loans-mortgages/090716/

Relevant Sources:

Soil Testing - WVU Extension - West Virginia University - https://extension.wvu.edu/natural-resources/soil-water/soil-testing

A Practical Guide to Understanding Zoning Laws - https://propertymetrics.com/blog/zoning-laws/

How to Finance Your Homestead — https://homesteadingfamily.com/how-to-finance-your-homestead/

Identifying and Predicting Environmental Impacts - https://www.researchgate.net/publication/27478544_The_Science_of_Assessment_Identifying_and_Predicting_Environmental_Impacts

How to Improve Garden Soil With Amendments - https://www.thespruce.com/making-good-soil-out-of-bad-1402428

Living Off-Grid: Homesteading 101

Chapter 2
Designing and Building a Sustainable Home

Imagine your home as a leaf, effortlessly floating on the gentle current of a stream. It's a natural extension of the environment, coexisting with the ebb and flow of the seasons, the warmth of the sun, and the nurturing rain. This home is more than a shelter—it's a living, breathing space that blends seamlessly into the landscape, minimizing its footprint while maximizing comfort and efficiency. That, my friends, is the heart of eco-friendly home design.

In this chapter, we'll explore a variety of sustainable home designs that do more than just stand against the elements—they embrace them. These structures are the embodiment of innovation, shaped by the hands of those who dare to think differently about the way we live. They are testaments to the fact that our homes can be both sanctuaries for our families and stewards of the Earth.

Overview of Eco-Friendly Home Design

Passive Solar Design

When the sun rises, it doesn't just bring light; it brings energy. Passive solar design is all about capturing and converting that energy and putting it to work in heating and lighting your home. The concept is simple: position your home so that it gets maximum sun exposure during the winter and minimal direct sunlight during the summer. It's about working with the sun's path, not against it.

Materials with high thermal mass, like concrete or brick, are used within the home to absorb and store the sun's warmth during the day and release it at night. This is like wearing a black t-shirt on a sunny day; it absorbs heat. When you're in the sun the absorption of the sun keeps you warm, until you decide to step into the shade. Large, south-facing windows let in sunlight, which is then trapped by insulated window coverings at night to keep the warmth from escaping.

Passive solar design is as much about preventing heat loss as it is about gaining heat. Proper insulation, strategic shading, and airtight construction ensure that once the heat is in, it stays in. This not only reduces your reliance on external heating sources but also cuts down on energy costs.

Earth Sheltered Homes

Earth-sheltered homes take 'getting back to nature' to a new level. You are literally building into the earth. By building into the earth, you are monopolizing on the soil's natural insulating properties. The earth acts as a thermal buffer, keeping the home warmer in winter and cooler in summer. It's like being hugged by the land itself—the temperature fluctuations inside the home are minimal, no matter what Mother Nature is up to outside.

These homes can be built partially or fully underground, with roofs that are often covered with soil and vegetation. They blend into the landscape, which not only minimizes their visual impact but also provides extra insulation. Plus, the earth covering protects against wind, rain, and even fire. It's a fortress, but one that works with the environment rather than barricading against it.

Some of the disadvantages of living underground include there is very little natural light, no outdoor or patio space, it's likely to be damp and have mold/moisture issues and flooding may be a potential problem, depending where you live.

Straw Bale Construction

Straw bale construction brings a touch of the pastoral to modern living. The bales—stacked and then plastered with clay, lime, or cement—provide exceptional insulation. Straw is a byproduct of grain farming, so using it as a building material repurposes what might otherwise go to waste. Think of it like making a quilt from leftover fabric scraps—resourceful and cozy.

Designing and Building a Sustainable Home

A straw bale wall has a high R-value, which measures resistance to heat flow. The higher the R-value, the better the insulation. Plus, straw bale construction has a certain aesthetic charm, with thick walls and deep window seats that invite you to sit, read, and sip a cup of tea while looking out over your homestead.

The disadvantages of straw bale construction are that it is very susceptible to rodent infestations, and moisture related problems due to inadequate roof overhangs, flashing, plumbing condensation. Also, there might be difficulties in obtaining insurance and financing for this type of structure.

Tiny Homes

The tiny home movement isn't just about adorable houses on wheels—it's a statement on living sustainably. These compact abodes force us to consider what we truly need in terms of space and possessions. By downsizing, the environmental impact is minimized. Less building material is required, less land is disturbed, and less energy is used to heat and cool the space.

Tiny homes can be fixed to a permanent location or mobile. Mobile tiny homes, about the same size as a 400 square foot recreational vehicle, permit chasing the perfect climate, reduce commuting, or even share land with others in a communal setting. It's a versatile solution that challenges the notion that bigger is always better. Tiny homes show us that when it comes to creating a sustainable, fulfilling life, sometimes less is indeed more.

The downside of tiny homes includes the lack of storage space, you can cannot use full size appliances, and having company over may be cramped each room is multi-tasked.

Planning Your Sustainable Home

To bring these concepts to life, let's visualize a day in a home designed with these principles in mind:

- **Morning:** The sun peeks over the horizon, casting rays through your south-facing windows. The light bounces off the thermal mass floor, slowly warming the space as you enjoy your morning coffee.
- **Afternoon:** As the day heats up, overhangs and deciduous trees shade your windows, keeping the interior cool. The earth-sheltered part of your home maintains a steady temperature, offering relief from the midday heat.

- **Evening:** The sun sets, and your home begins to release the stored heat from the day. The straw bale walls hold the warmth, providing a cozy atmosphere for the night ahead.
- **Night:** With the temperature dropping outside, your tiny home retains its comfort, requiring minimal energy to stay warm. You sleep soundly, knowing your home is in harmony with the natural world.

Incorporating these eco-friendly design elements means thinking beyond the conventional. It's about seeing your home as part of a larger ecosystem and making choices that benefit both your family and the environment. As we continue to build and shape our living spaces, remember that sustainability isn't just a buzzword—it's a blueprint for the future.

Material Selection for Sustainability

Selecting the right materials for your home is like setting the stage for a lifelong performance. Every board, every nail, every swath of fabric plays a role in the tale of sustainability your dwelling will tell. The choices you make now echo through the years, shaping not just the aesthetic of your home but its ecological footprint as well.

Reclaimed Materials

The use of reclaimed materials is a nod to both history and efficiency. Imagine giving new life to wood from a century-old barn or bricks from a historic factory. These materials carry with them a patina of the past while sparing the resources and energy that new production would entail. Reclaimed wood can find new purpose as flooring, beams, or even as the framing for your sustainable home. Each piece tells a story, and together, they write a narrative of conservation.

Reclaimed metal roofing, with its resilience and longevity, is another example. It weathers over time to a beautiful patina and provides a durable shelter that withstands the elements. By choosing reclaimed materials, you reduce landfill waste and cut down on the environmental impact of manufacturing and transporting new materials.

Locally Sourced Timber

When the topic turns to timber, the adage "think globally, act locally" couldn't be more apt. Locally sourced timber minimizes the carbon dioxide

Designing and Building a Sustainable Home

emissions associated with long-distance transportation. Moreover, it supports the local economy and often comes from sustainably managed forests where the health of the ecosystem is a priority.

Consider the species of trees that thrive in your region. They are naturally suited to the climate and conditions, which means they'll stand up better to the local weather patterns and pests. This local timber not only grounds your home in its environment but also creates a smaller carbon footprint from the outset.

Natural Insulation Materials

Insulation is the silent sentinel of your home's energy efficiency. Natural insulation materials, such as sheep's wool, cotton, or cellulose, provide a cozy barrier against the cold and heat without introducing harmful chemicals or relying on fossil fuels. Sheep's wool is a remarkable insulator. Its fibers are naturally crimped, creating tiny air pockets that trap heat, much like a down jacket.

Cellulose, often made from recycled newspapers, is another eco-friendly option. It's treated with a natural fire retardant and can be densely packed into walls, attics, and floors, sealing your home from drafts and temperature swings. These materials breathe, regulating humidity and contributing to healthier indoor air quality.

Low-VOC Paints

The finishing touches to your home should protect and beautify without compromising the air you breathe. Low-VOC (volatile organic compound) paints fulfill this role very well. Traditional paints release chemicals into the air, not just during application but for years afterward. Low-VOC alternatives, on the other hand, have reduced levels of these harmful emissions.

Additionally, these paints are less taxing on the environment in their production and disposal. They often come in a broad range of colors that continue to expand, proving that eco-friendly doesn't mean sacrificing style. With low-VOC paints, the walls your home can radiate color and character, minus the environmental and health costs.

As you select materials for your sustainable home, think of them as the threads in a tapestry. Each choice weaves into the next, creating a picture that is both beautiful and responsible. The materials you choose are as integral to your home as the roots are to a tree, grounding it in the principles of sustainability and stewardship.

Energy Efficiency in Home Construction

When the chill of winter or the heat of summer knocks on your door, a well-designed home should stand as a guardian, regulating the indoor climate while keeping energy consumption to a minimum. It's here, in the construction phase, that energy efficiency becomes the cornerstone of a sustainable home. From the insulation in the walls to the glass in the windows, every element plays a role in maintaining a comfortable, energy-efficient living space.

Insulation and Weatherization

Think of insulation as the warm, protective blanket that wraps around your home, keeping the cozy in and the cold out. High-quality insulation in the walls, floors, and attic is a must for an energy-efficient home. It reduces the need for heating and cooling systems to work overtime, thereby saving energy and reducing utility bills. But insulation is just one piece of the puzzle.

Weatherization seals the deal. Literally, this means meticulously sealing cracks and gaps where air might escape, adding weather-stripping around doors and windows, and using caulk to fill any openings where different building materials meet. It's a detail-oriented process, but one that pays dividends in the form of a more controlled internal environment and significant energy savings.

Energy-Efficient Windows

Windows are the eyes of a home, offering views of the outside world while playing a significant role in energy efficiency. Double or triple-paned windows filled with inert gas and coated with heat-reflective films create a barrier against temperature extremes. They keep the summer heat at bay and retain precious warmth when the temperatures drop.

The frames matter too. Materials like fiberglass, vinyl, or treated wood add to the windows' insulative properties, further contributing to a home's energy efficiency. Investing in these energy-efficient windows might come with a higher initial cost, but the reduction in energy bills and the increase in comfort level are truly worth it.

Passive Solar Heating

Passive solar heating involves the strategic placement of thermal mass materials that capture and store the sun's heat during the day, releasing it gradually as temperatures decline. These materials, including concrete, brick, stone, and water, possess the inherent property to absorb, store, and later release thermal energy.

This approach involves considering the building's layout, insulation, and window placement to maximize natural heating and cooling and requires a thoughtful balance—too much glass on the wrong side of the house could lead to overheating or energy loss. But with careful planning, passive solar heating can significantly reduce the need for artificial heating, drawing on the sun's natural warmth to keep the home comfortable.

Natural Cooling Techniques

As summer takes center stage, natural cooling techniques step into the spotlight, ensuring your home remains a cool retreat without heavy reliance on air conditioning. These techniques are a blend of smart design and natural phenomena. For instance, orienting the home to catch prevailing breezes, incorporating ventilated roofing, and using shading devices like pergolas or overhangs to block high-angle summer sun.

Inside, materials with thermal mass, which were so adept at storing heat in the winter, now help to absorb indoor heat during the day, releasing it at night when the air is cooler. Additionally, planting deciduous trees provides shade in summer while allowing sunlight to warm the home in winter when their leaves have fallen.

Putting these energy-efficient strategies into action during the construction phase sets the stage for a home that not only stands up to the elements but also respects them. The goal is a living space that maintains a comfortable atmosphere year-round, with minimal energy input—an environment that not only shelters but also preserves.

Balancing Comfort and Sustainability

Creating a homestead that's both comfortable and sustainable is like composing a melody where each note contributes to a harmonious melody. It's about finding the perfect pitch between eco-friendly practices and a lifestyle that wraps you in warmth and well-being. In this section, we focus on the elements that transform a house into a home without sacrificing our commitment to the planet.

Space Utilization

Efficient use of space in your home is akin to a well-orchestrated dance, where every step is purposeful, and every movement is fluid. The key lies in designing multi-functional areas that adapt to changing needs—a dining area that doubles as a workspace, a loft that serves as both a sleeping nook and storage haven, or a living room that can host gatherings or transform into a tranquil retreat. When your rooms can multi-task, then it's almost as if you have twice the house. At least you do in functionality.

Incorporating built-in furniture or fold-away features maximizes space and minimizes clutter. This approach not only serves the immediate functional needs but also reduces the environmental impact by limiting the necessity for more building materials and furniture. Space efficiency goes hand-in-hand with minimalism, encouraging a lifestyle that values quality over quantity and design over excess.

Indoor Air Quality

The air within your sanctuary should be as fresh as the breeze that rustles through the leaves outside. This is achieved not just by avoiding materials that off-gas harmful chemicals, but also by integrating systems that foster constant airflow and filter out pollutants. Consider a heat recovery ventilator (HRV) system, which provides a continuous supply of fresh air, conserving energy while maintaining a healthy indoor atmosphere.

Indoor plants are also natural allies in this endeavor, acting as living air purifiers that absorb toxins and emit oxygen. A thoughtful selection of indoor greenery can enhance both air quality and the aesthetic appeal of your home, bringing a piece of the outside world into your living space.

Natural Lighting

The glow of natural light brings a home to life, reducing the need for artificial lighting and creating an ambiance that changes with the rhythm of the day. Skylights and strategically placed windows invite daylight to pour into your home, brightening every corner and lifting spirits. Consider translucent materials for internal doors or walls to allow light to filter through the home, maintaining privacy while sharing light across spaces.

The planning of window placement is crucial—north-facing windows, for instance, provide consistent, indirect light that illuminates without the heat of direct sun exposure. With the right balance, natural light can be the main source of lighting during the day, cutting down on electricity usage and forging a connection with the world outside.

Smart Water Usage

Effective water management is crucial for off-grid living, from collection to usage and recycling. Rainwater harvesting systems can be designed to blend with your home's esthetics while providing vital water source. Gray water systems can recycle water from sinks and showers for use in gardens, reducing overall water consumption. Implementing water efficient fixtures and appliances is a simple, yet impactful way to conserve water. Low flow toilets, shower heads, and faucet aerators can significantly cut down on water usage without sacrificing performance. Energy-star rated appliances like dishwashers and washing machines are designed for efficiency and can save water and electricity.

What Size House is Comfortable?

The basic room types needed in a home include: a living room, bedroom, bathroom and kitchen, using multiples of 8 for 8-foot wood studs a 16 by 24-foot space could accommodate a living room and dining area. A 16 by 24-foot space may include the kitchen and a washer and dryer. A 16 by 16-foot space could become a bedroom with closet and the bathroom could measure in at 8 feet by 8 feet. Hallways and storage areas need to be included in the overall floor plan.If it's possible to dig a basement, a partially finished basement can double for a storm shelter and root cellar. While the other half could store the solar batteries and rainwater collection system. And, for finishing touches, a north and west facing outdoor porch provides nice "breathing room" for three seasons.

This quickly adds up to 1200 square feet for a one-bedroom house. The size for additional bedrooms at 16 by 16-feet, or 256 sq.ft. per bedroom allows room for closets and study areas. Using round numbers; a 2-bedroom house becomes 1500 sq ft and a 3-bedroom house becomes 1800 sq. ft., etc.

Outdoor Living Spaces

Outdoor living spaces are the bridges that connect the comfort of your home to the natural world. Decks, patios, or porches extend your living area into the outdoors, offering spots for relaxation, dining, or simply enjoying the view. These areas encourage a lifestyle that appreciates the open air and integrates the environment into daily life.

The design of these spaces takes into account the direction of wind, sun, and views, creating an oasis that is protected from harsh weather while capturing the best aspects of your surroundings. Using sustainable, durable materials ensures these outdoor areas can be enjoyed for years to come without frequent replacements or repairs.

In crafting spaces that merge comfort with ecological consciousness, the true essence of a sustainable home is realized. It is a place of refuge that not only shelters and nurtures its inhabitants but also pays homage to the environment that cradles it. The balance struck within these walls and in these outdoor spaces is a testament to the fact that living sustainably does not mean sacrificing the joys and comforts of home.

As we wrap up this exploration of sustainable home construction, it's clear that the journey to a greener, more self-sufficient life is filled with opportunities for innovation and creativity. The choices we make in designing our homes are reflections of our values and our hopes for the future—a future where sustainability and comfort coexist, where the homes we build are as kind to the earth as they are to those who dwell within them.

And so, with these principles set firmly in our minds, we turn our gaze to the next chapter, where we'll uncover the mysteries of harnessing the power of the sun. The radiant energy that fuels life on our planet can also power our homes, and understanding how to tap into this abundant resource is a vital step in our homesteading journey. The sun's rays, once perceived as merely the bringer of dawn, become the catalyst for a home that hums with the pulse of sustainable energy.

References:

21 Construction Techniques to Build a Small, Sustainable Eco-Friendly Home - https://www.foxblocks.com/blog/eco-friendly-home

7 Eco-friendly Insulation Alternatives for a Green Home - https://inhabitat.com/7-eco-friendly-insulation-alternatives-for-a-green-home/

Passive Solar Homes - https://www.energy.gov/energysaver/passive-solar-homes

Improving Air Quality Ventilation Strategies in Energy-Efficient - https://utilitiesone.com/improving-air-quality-ventilation-strategies-in-energy-efficient-building-envelopes

Straw Bale Home Basics - https://www.nachi.org/straw-bale-home-basics-history.htm

Relevant Resources:

20+ Sustainable Building Materials in 2023: https://gbdmagazine.com/sustainable-building-materials/

Passive Solar Design - Sustainability - Williams College: https://sustainability.williams.edu/green-building-basics/passive-solar-design/

Rainwater Harvesting System Design, Installation, & - https://www.watercache.com/rainwater

ENERGY STAR Most Efficient 2024 - https://www.energystar.gov/products/most_efficient

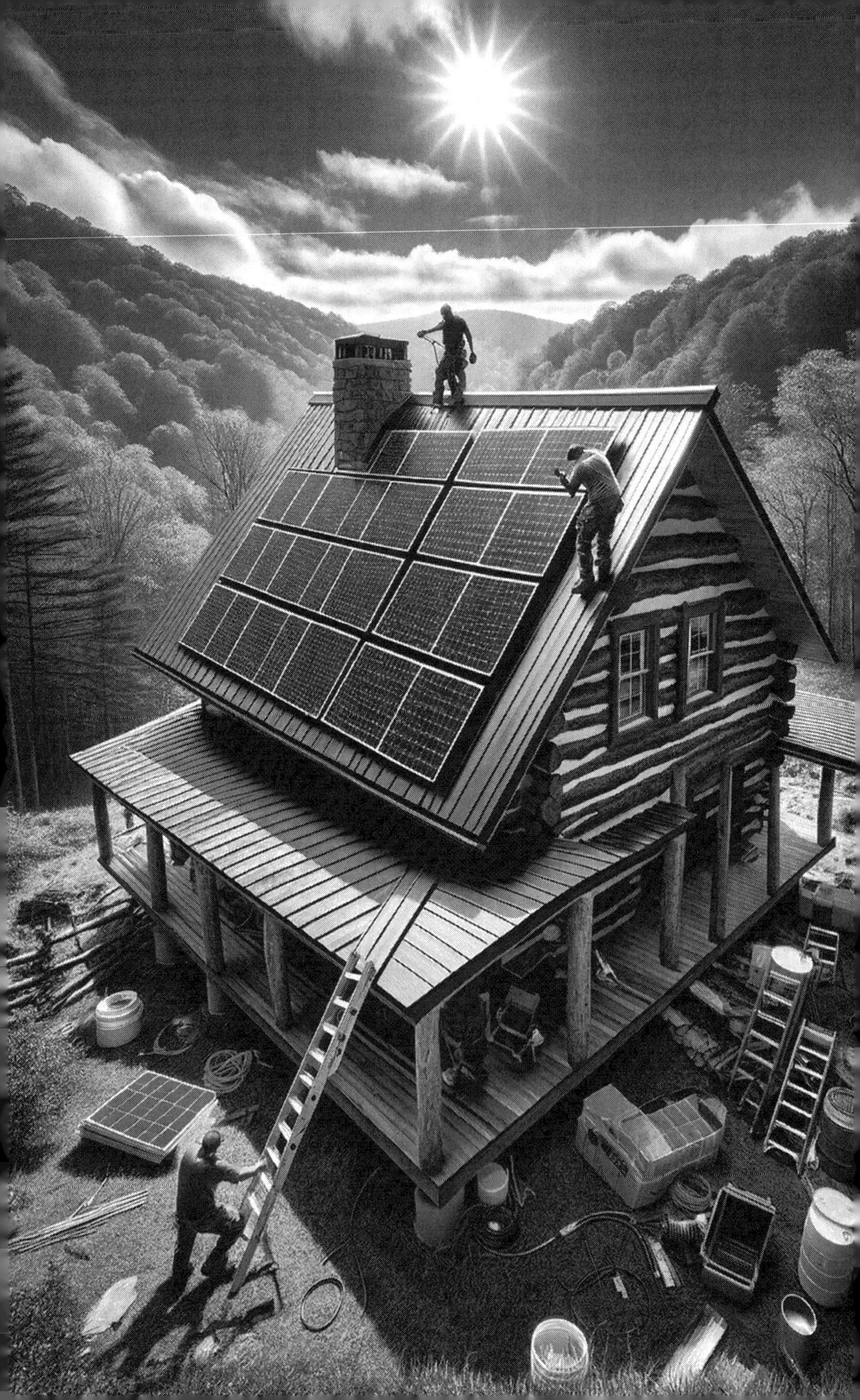

Chapter 3
Solar Power Simplified

The sun peeks over the horizon, and a new day begins. It's a familiar sight that has greeted humankind since the dawn of time. But there's a twist here—those first golden rays that touch the earth are more than just the heralds of morning; they're the bearers of energy, vast and untapped. Step outside, feel the warmth on your face, and know this: the same sunlight that helps the garden grow and gives us those perfect summer days is ready and waiting to power your home. It's not science fiction; it's solar power, and it's surging forward, ready to revolutionize the way we live.

In this chapter, we're not just talking about solar energy; we're rolling up our sleeves and getting to grips with it. You'll find no jargon-laden lectures here—just clear, practical insights that turn the complexity of solar energy into something as straightforward and approachable as planting your first backyard tomato. So let's shed some light on the basics of solar power, and before you know it, you'll be soaking up that sun in a whole new way.

The Basics of Solar Power

Understanding Photovoltaics

Photovoltaics (PV) might sound like a term reserved for lab-coated scientists, but it's actually quite down-to-earth. It's the process that converts sunlight directly into electricity, and it's at the heart of most home solar power systems. PV technology is not just about catching a few rays; it's like a sunflower field turning its collective gaze to the sun, each flower (or solar

Living Off-Grid: Homesteading 101

cell, in our case) working to convert light into a form of energy that can fuel everything from your morning coffee pot to your nighttime reading lamp.

Here's how photovoltaics work in a nutshell: each solar cell is made with materials that contain electrons, which get excited when they're hit by photons from sunlight. This excitement creates an electrical current. Think of it like a busy coffee shop in the morning—sunlight is the caffeine that gets everything moving. The electrical current is then harnessed and directed to power your home's electrical systems. It's a clean, renewable process that happens silently on your rooftop, requiring no moving parts and releasing no emissions into the atmosphere.

Solar Power System Components

A solar power system is like a symphony—each component plays a critical role, and when they work together in harmony, the result is beautiful. Here are the key players:

- **Solar Panels:** These are the front-line troops, capturing sunlight and converting it into direct current (DC) electricity. They're the most visible part of the system, usually mounted on your roof or on poles in a sunny part on your property.

- **Inverter:** This device is like a translator, taking the DC electricity from the panels and turning it into alternating current (AC) electricity, which is what powers most homes in the United States.

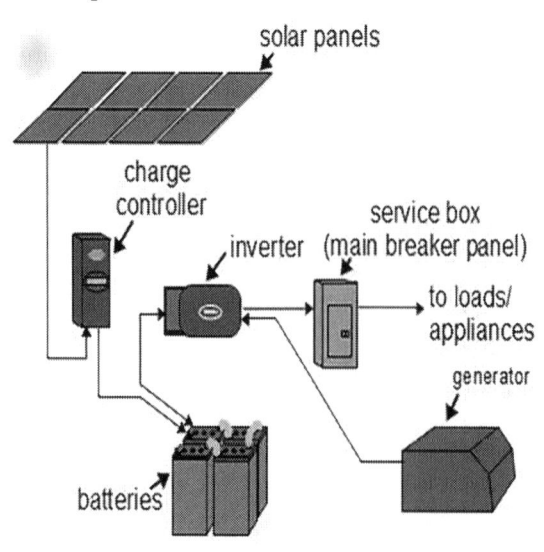

- **Battery Storage (optional):** Batteries store energy for when the sun isn't shining—like a squirrel stashing nuts for the winter. They're not essential for all solar power systems, but they're becoming more popular as folks look to store their own energy.
- **Charge Controller:** Consider this the traffic cop of the system, directing the flow of electricity to the batteries and preventing overcharging.
- **Electrical Panel:** This is the hub where the AC electricity is distributed to the various circuits in your home.
- **Utility Meter:** If your system is tied to the grid, this meter will track your energy production and usage. In many places, if you produce more energy than you use, the meter will actually run backward, earning you credits with the utility company.
- **Disconnect Switches:** Safety first! These switches allow you to shut down the system for maintenance or in case of an emergency.

Imagine your solar power system like a team working on a home renovation. Each member has a specific skill set, essential for the project's success. The solar panels are your builders, the inverter is your project manager, and the battery storage is your savings account for a rainy day. The charge controller ensures everyone's safety on-site, the electrical panel organizes the distribution of tasks, the utility meter keeps the budget in check, and the disconnect switches are your emergency exits.

How Solar Energy Works

The sun's energy flows to earth and hits your solar panels, beginning the process of converting light to electricity. It's a journey from the panels through the inverter and into your home's electrical system. When the sun is up and your system is producing more energy than you need, you might be sending power back to the grid, spinning your meter backward, or storing the excess in batteries for later use.

Consider this scenario: it's a sunny day, and you're at work. Your solar panels are soaking up sunlight, your inverter is hard at work, and your home is running on this clean energy. The dishwasher is humming, the fridge keeps your food cool, and if you have a battery system, it's storing power for later. Then, you come home in the evening, and even though the sun has set, your lights and appliances can still run off the solar energy you collected during the day.

The beauty of solar energy is in its simplicity and reliability. While the science behind it might seem complex, the day-to-day operation is straightforward. You're using a resource that's been around for billions of years and will continue to shine on us for billions more. It's no wonder that more and more folks are turning their gaze to the sky and tapping into the clean, sustainable power of the sun. With solar energy, you're not just cutting down on utility bills; you're becoming a part of a global shift towards a greener future.

Installation and Maintenance of Solar Panel Systems

Site Assessment for Solar Installation

The leap into solar begins with a clear understanding of your property's potential to catch those golden rays. An effective site assessment is the map that will guide you. A professional walks the land, eyes keen for details that affect solar gain, such as orientation, shading, and the angle of your roof. This step is vital; it's about ensuring the sun's path intersects with your panels as often as possible throughout the day.

Factors like the pitch of your roof, the direction it faces, and any nearby trees or structures that might cast a shadow come into play. The goal is to identify the prime location where your panels will receive maximum sunlight exposure. The assessment may reveal that ground mounting in an open field is preferable to a roof setup, or perhaps your roof is the perfect stage for your solar array.

Your property's geography is also a consideration. In the Northern Hemisphere, south-facing roofs are ideal. The tilt angle is fine-tuned to the latitude of your location, optimizing the angle at which your panels sit to greet the sun. For those in urban settings or with less-than-ideal solar conditions, don't fret. Innovations in panel efficiency mean that even non-optimal sites can still yield substantial energy.

Solar Panel Mounting Techniques

With the stage set, it's time to secure your solar panels. Mounting techniques vary, each with its own merits. Roof mounts are popular, keeping the panels high, where they are more likely to meet the sun unobstructed. Consideration for the roof's condition is essential – it should be in good repair to bear the weight and future lifespan of the solar array.

Solar Power Simplified

Ground mounts take a different approach; they stake a claim to a sunny spot on your land. These installations allow for easier cleaning and maintenance, and they can be adjusted to the optimal angle independent of your home's orientation. Pole mounts hoist the panels even higher, potentially above obstacles like trees or buildings, and can include tracking systems that rotate the panels to follow the sun's arc, capturing more light than static stationary panels.

The method you choose balances aesthetics, space, and energy needs. It's about what works best for your homestead, your budget, and your energy goals. Installers anchor the panels to withstand the whims of Mother Nature, ensuring they stay put through storms and seasonal changes. The right mounting choice adds to the efficiency of your system and the harmony of your homestead's design.

Regular Maintenance Tasks for Solar Panels

Once your solar panels are in place, their upkeep is refreshingly low-key. These sun catchers are resilient, designed to withstand the elements, but they perform best with some regular attention. Keep an eye on them, just as you would any other part of your home.

The occasional cleaning ensures they operate at peak efficiency. Dust, leaves, or snow can act as a blanket, shading the cells from the sun. A gentle wash with water and a non-abrasive brush removes any accumulated grime. In snowy climates, a roof rake designed for solar panels can clear the white stuff without scratching the surface.

Monitoring is another piece of the maintenance puzzle. Many systems include apps or dashboards that allow you to watch your energy production in real-time. A sudden drop might signal that it's time for a check-up. The inverter, the system's heartbeat, usually has indicator lights that show its health status. If they suggest trouble, a certified technician can diagnose and resolve issues, often before they escalate.

Yearly inspections by a professional keeps things running smoothly. They'll tighten connections, verify that mounts are secure, and ensure that trees haven't grown to overshadow your panels. It's preventive care, much like visiting the doctor, but for your solar panel system. This ongoing maintenance ensures that your investment continues to pay dividends, both in energy for your home and in benefits for the environment.

Cost Benefit Analysis of Solar Energy

Initial Investment and Installation Costs

Stepping into the world of solar energy requires an upfront financial commitment. The sum total can influence your decision, so let's break it down. The initial investment combines the cost of solar panels, inverters, batteries (for those opting for storage), and the cost of labor for installation. Each element carries its own price, influenced by brand, quality, and capacity.

Picture this: you're shopping for a car. You have options from a no-frills compact to a luxury SUV with all the bells and whistles. Solar setups are similar. You can start small, with a modest array sufficient for basic needs, or go all out with a system that powers your entire homestead and then some. The choice you make aligns with both your energy demands and your financial plan.

It's not just the equipment and installation you're investing in; it's also the potential for federal, state, or local incentives. These financial boosts can take forms such as tax credits, rebates, or grants, slicing a portion off the total cost. It pays to research and apply for these incentives, as they can significantly lessen the initial financial blow.

Long-term Savings and Return on Investment

Flip the coin, and on the other side, you'll find the long-term savings that solar energy promises. Monthly utility bills shrink or may even disappear, depending on your system's size and your energy consumption. It's a pleasant side effect of your solar investment—the joy of watching your power meter tick backward on sunny days as you feed energy back into the grid, if that's an option available to you.

The return on investment (ROI) is not immediate but unfolds over time. It's a gradual recouping of costs as savings accumulate. The tipping point—the moment when savings outweigh the initial investment—varies. Factors like your home's energy efficiency, the cost of electricity in your area, and the size of your solar setup all play their part. But rest assured, the scales will eventually tip in your favor, marking the point where your solar system starts paying dividends.

It's prudent to consider the lifespan of your solar components. Panels come with warranties often guaranteeing output for up to 25 years, while inverters may need replacement sooner. Including these future costs in your calculations paints a more accurate picture of ROI. Yet, even with these considerations, solar energy remains a wise financial choice for many, offering a return that extends beyond mere dollars and cents.

Environmental Impact and Carbon Footprint Reduction

The choice to adopt solar energy resonates beyond the boundaries of your property. It's a personal step that has a global impact. The environmental impact of converting to solar is profound. You're reducing the reliance on fossil fuels, the culprits behind greenhouse gas emissions, that drive climate change. Every kilowatt-hour of solar-generated electricity is a step away from carbon-dioxide-emitting energy sources.

Your homestead becomes more than just a place to live; it transforms into an active participant in the fight against global warming. Consider the average carbon footprint of a household, a culmination of activities from driving to heating. By shifting to solar, you're effectively erasing a large swath of that footprint, replacing it with clean, renewable energy.

The sun's energy is abundant and inexhaustible, unlike the waning reserves of coal, oil, and natural gas. In utilizing this resource, you're contributing to a sustainable energy model, one that can be replicated and adopted worldwide. The transition to clean energy sources is critical in mitigating the worst effects of climate change, and your decision to go solar places you at the forefront of this shift.

As solar technology advances, the efficiency of panels improves, further enhancing their environmental benefits. The industry strides forward with innovations that reduce the use of hazardous materials and increase recyclability. Your investment in solar today supports an industry that is evolving towards an even greener future.

The benefits of solar energy, both financial and environmental, are clear. The initial costs are balanced by significant savings and a generous ROI over time. The positive impact on the environment is undeniable, offering a substantial reduction in your carbon footprint. As you weigh the costs against the benefits, consider not only the immediate effects on your budget but also the long-lasting implications for our planet. With solar energy, you're not just saving money; you're investing in a cleaner, more sustainable future for generations to come.

Troubleshooting Common Solar Power Issues

Solar panels, inverters, and batteries are the trusty stalwarts of your solar system, quietly doing their job day in, day out. But like any well-oiled machine, they may occasionally hiccup. Not to worry—most issues have simple fixes, and understanding how to address these common snags will keep your system in tip-top shape.

Dealing with Reduced Power Output

Sometimes, you might notice that your solar panels aren't producing as much power as they used to. It's like a seasoned runner suddenly slowing down—it's noticeable and needs attention. First, check for the obvious: is there anything blocking the panels? Fallen leaves, bird droppings, or even a buildup of dust can create a barrier between the panels and the sunlight they crave.

Next, look at the weather. Cloudy days are the introverts of the weather world—they don't like to make a scene, but they can still impact your solar output. If the skies have been gray, you may just need to wait for the sun to come out again. However, if the weather's been fine and your panels are clean, it could be a sign of aging. Solar panels do lose a bit of efficiency each year—it's a natural part of their lifecycle. If they're older, it might be time to consider replacing them or adding more to your array to make up for lost power.

Handling Solar Inverter Issues

The inverter is the brain of your solar system, and sometimes it needs a bit of troubleshooting. If you see error messages or notice the inverter switching off unexpectedly, it's time to play detective. A common culprit is a simple one: the inverter might just need a reset. Like giving your computer a reboot, this can often clear up the issue.

Temperature can also affect your inverter. If it's too hot, the inverter might overheat and shut down to protect itself. Make sure it's in a spot with good ventilation, away from direct sunlight. If it's too cold, on the other hand, the inverter might struggle to start up. Check the manufacturer's temperature guidelines to make sure your inverter is operating within the recommended range.

Solar Power Simplified

Sometimes, the inverter might be fine, but it's not getting the power it needs from the panels. This could be due to a wiring problem or an issue with the panels themselves. Check the connections to make sure they're secure and look for any signs of damage. If everything looks good, but the problem persists, it might be time to call in a professional.

Addressing Battery and Charge Controller Problems

Batteries and charge controllers are like the heart and lungs of your off-grid solar system, storing the energy and managing its flow. If you notice your batteries aren't holding a charge as they should, the first step is to check their age. Batteries have a finite lifespan, and after several years of service, they might not be able to store energy as efficiently.

If age isn't the issue, consider the depth of discharge. Draining your batteries too low can shorten their life. A charge controller ensures that your batteries stay within a healthy charging range. If your batteries are frequently over or undercharged, the charge controller might need adjustment or replacement.

Sometimes, the issue is simply a matter of maintenance. Batteries require regular check-ups. For flooded lead-acid batteries, this means checking water levels and topping them off with distilled water if needed. Keeping the terminals clean and tight ensures a good connection and proper charging.

If your system uses a different type of battery, like lithium-ion or gel, follow the manufacturer's guidelines for care. They generally require less maintenance but still benefit from regular inspections to ensure everything is functioning as it should.

With these troubleshooting tips, you can ensure your solar power system continues to provide clean, renewable energy to your homestead. Keeping an eye out for issues and addressing them promptly will help maintain the longevity and efficiency of your setup. Remember, most problems have straight-forward solutions, and a little bit of knowledge goes a long way in keeping your solar system shining bright.

As we look back on our solar journey thus far, it's clear that the path to energy independence is both rewarding and manageable. From the initial steps of understanding the basics to the finer points of maintenance and troubleshooting, we've equipped ourselves with the knowledge to navigate

Living Off-Grid: Homesteading 101

the occasional bumps in the road. Each solution we apply reinforces our connection to the natural world and our commitment to sustainability. With our solar systems humming along, we turn our attention to the next chapter in our homesteading adventure, where we'll explore the vast potential of harnessing not just the power of the sun, but also the strength of the wind and the flow of water, expanding our renewable energy repertoire.

References:

Solar Energy Basics - https://www.nrel.gov/research/re-solar.html

Best Practices for Solar Operations and Maintenance - https://www.ciservicesinc.com/best-practices-for-solar-operations-and-maintenance/

Economics of Solar Photovoltaic Systems - https://extensionpublications.unl.edu/assets/html/g2182/build/g2182.htm

Solar System Fault Finding Guide & Solutions - https://www.cleanenergyreviews.info/blog/guide-solar-panel-problems-fault-finding

Relevant Resources:

Shining Light on Five Top Solar Trends of 2023 - https://www.smeinc.com/news-events/article/shining-light-on-five-top-solar-trends-of-2023/

DIY Solar Energy: A Step-by-Step Guide with Tips and Tricks for Installing a Home Photovoltaic System by John Patterson

As PV Market Evolved in the Last Year, Prices Went Up – Prices Went Down - https://www.nrel.gov/news/program/2023/as-pv-market-evolved-in-the-last-year-prices-went-up-prices-went-down.html

Do Solar Panels Increase Your Home's Value? - https://www.forbes.com/home-improvement/solar/does-solar-increase-home-value/

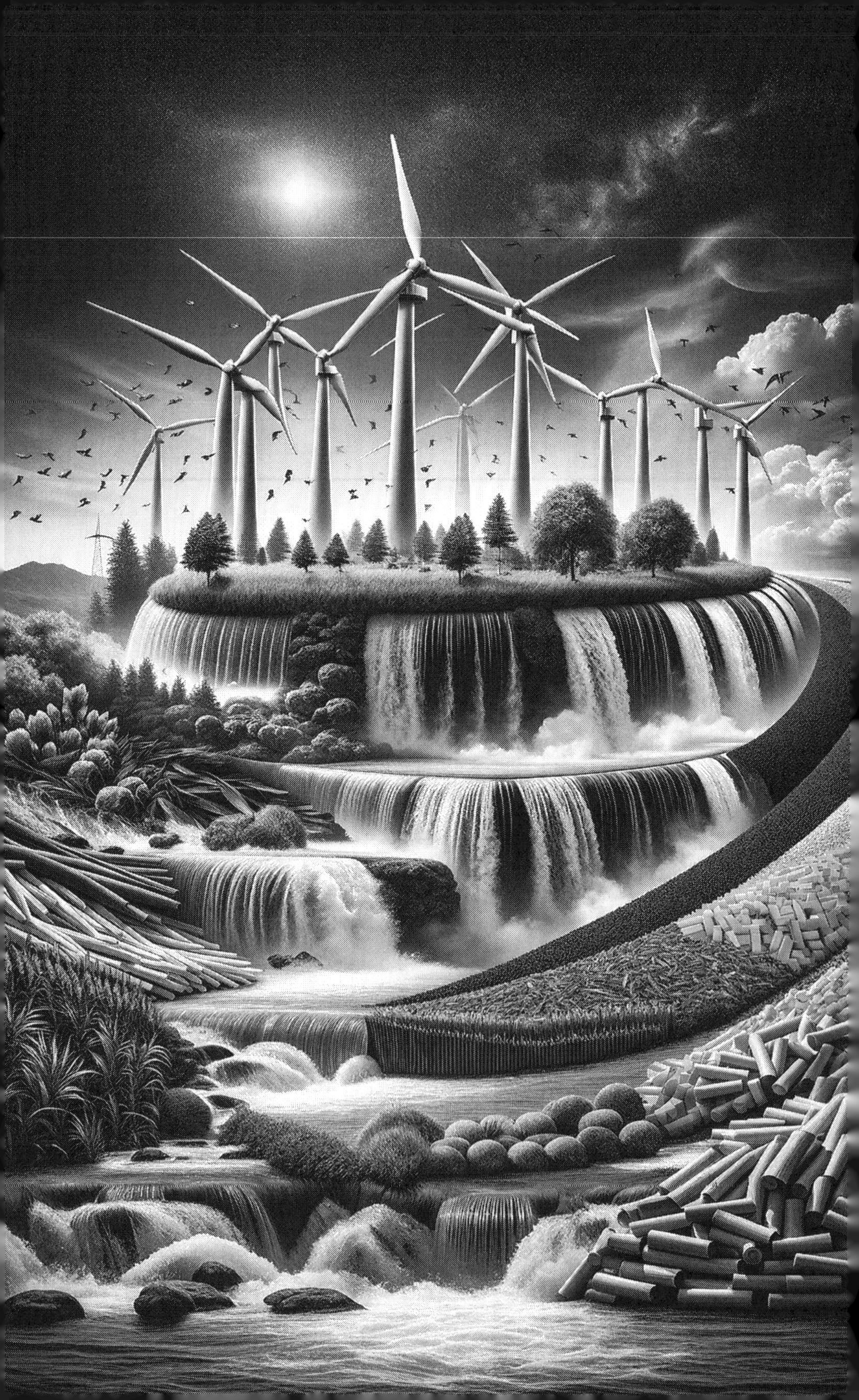

Chapter 4

Exploring Alternative Energy Sources

Picture this: a crisp morning on your homestead, the dew still fresh on the grass, and the leaves rustling gently in the breeze. That breeze—have you ever stopped to consider its untamed potential? It's more than just a pleasant coolness on your skin; it's a force of nature that's been shaping landscapes and powering journeys for millennia. Now, it's knocking at your door, offering a treasure trove of energy, ripe for the taking.

Here on your homestead, where every gust of wind rustles through the trees and brushes past your barn, you stand at the threshold of an energy revolution. Wind, an ancient traveler of the world's airways, is ready to settle down on your land and put down roots, converting its kinetic energy into a steady, reliable source of power. So, let's roll out the welcome mat and get to know the ins and outs of harnessing this breezy friend bearing gifts.

Wind Power Basics

Understanding Wind Turbines

Wind turbines are modern-day windmills, sleek and efficient. They're like the tall, silent types at a party—unassuming yet captivating. But what really goes on inside these towering figures? It's a dance of physics: as the wind blows, it spins the turbine's blades around a rotor, which in turn spins a generator, and voilà—electricity is born. Its kinetic energy transformed into electrical energy, a seamless conversion that's as natural as breathing.

Living Off-Grid: Homesteading 101

The key components of a wind turbine are straightforward:

- Blades: They catch the wind, like sails on a ship.
- Rotor: Connected to the blades, it spins as they do.
- Generator: It converts the rotational motion into electricity.
- Tower: It elevates the turbine so it can catch stronger winds.
- Nacelle: Sitting atop the tower, it houses the generator and other key components.

Wind Speed and Power Generation

When it comes to wind power, speed is the name of the game. Think of wind speed like the flow of a river—the stronger the current, the more power you can generate. There's a sweet spot, however; too little wind and the turbine won't turn, too much and it might need to shut down to avoid damage.

Most turbines start producing power with winds at about 6 to 9 miles per hour, known as the 'cut-in speed'. Their optimum efficiency hits at higher speeds, which varies per model. But here's the catch—the power potential doesn't just increase linearly with wind speed; it's a cubic relationship (x^3), an exponential of three. That means if you double the wind speed, you might increase the power potential by up to eight times (2x2x2). This is why even a slight increase in wind speed can significantly boost your energy output.

Wind Turbine Placement Considerations

Planting a wind turbine isn't like planting corn—there's a bit more to consider. The right location can make all the difference between a trickle of energy and a steady flow. Here's what to keep in mind:

- **Height:** Air is thicker closer to the ground, which means more drag and less wind. By placing your turbine higher, you can tap into faster, less turbulent winds.
- **Open Space:** Wind flows more smoothly over open areas without obstructions like trees or buildings. Turbines love these open spaces—it's where they can breathe and perform their best.
- **Distance from Obstacles:** Speaking of breathing room, turbines need to be positioned at least 30 feet above anything within a 500-foot radius. This helps avoid turbulent air, which can decrease efficiency and increase wear on the turbine.

- **Local Wind Patterns:** Get to know your local wind patterns like you know your neighbors. Monitoring wind speed and direction over time can help you pinpoint the perfect spot for your turbine.

The Importance of Local Regulations and Community Relations

Before you go planting a turbine, there's paperwork to tend to. Local regulations may have a say on where and how you can install your wind energy system. It's best to check with your local government about zoning laws, permits, or any restrictions that might apply to your area.

And let's not forget about the human element—your community. Not everyone may be thrilled about your towering new friend. It's important to communicate with your neighbors, address concerns, and work together to find solutions that benefit everyone. After all, the wind is a shared resource, and tapping into it should be a collective win.

There you have it—the essentials of wind power for the homesteader. While we've covered the basics, the world of wind energy is as vast as the sky itself. There are more layers to uncover, more nuances to explore, but with this foundation, you're well on your way to capturing the wind's untamed energy and making it a cornerstone of your homestead's power supply.

Hydroelectric Power for Homesteaders

Imagine the gentle murmur of a stream coursing through your property, a sound as constant as the ticking of a clock. This stream, however, does more than provide a serene backdrop to your daily life; it's a dynamic source of energy, waiting to be tapped. Obviously, a homesteader isn't going to build Hoover Dam in their backyard, but micro-hydro systems offer an opportunity to convert the flow of water on your land into a steady stream of electricity, turning the timeless journey of water into a resource that lights up your home and powers your tools.

Basics of Micro-Hydro Systems

At its core, a micro-hydro system is a small-scale version of the massive hydroelectric dams that power whole cities. Yet, its humble size gives no indication of its real strength. This system relies on flowing water to spin a turbine connected to a generator, creating electricity. It's an old concept, dating back to waterwheels, but with a modern twist that maximizes efficiency and minimizes environmental impact.

Components of a micro-hydro system include:

- **Intake:** Where water is diverted from the stream.
- **Penstock:** A pipeline that channels the water to the turbine.
- **Turbine or Waterwheel:** The device that converts the energy of flowing water into mechanical energy.
- **Generator:** Which converts mechanical energy from the turbine into electricity.
- **Tailrace:** Where water is returned to the stream after passing through the turbine.
- **Controller:** Manages the flow of electricity from the generator to the batteries or the grid.

The beauty of a micro-hydro system lies in its ability to provide continuous, reliable power. Unlike solar or wind power, which depend on the sun shining or the wind blowing, a stream flows day and night, offering a more constant energy source.

Site Assessment for Hydroelectric Power

Selecting the right site for your micro-hydro system is a subtle blend of art and science. Here's where you'll need to become intimately familiar with the waterways on your property. Key factors to assess include:

- **Flow Rate:** The volume of water moving through a section of the stream per unit of time. A higher flow rate can mean more potential power.
- **Head:** The vertical drop of the stream over a certain distance. Greater head can lead to increased power output.
- **Accessibility:** The ease with which you can install and maintain the system components.
- **Environmental Impact:** Ensuring that your system doesn't harm local ecosystems or fish populations.
- **Land & Clay Resources to Dam a Retention Pond:** The capability to create a retention pond creating continuous water flow.

Exploring Alternative Energy Sources

A flow rate of 100 gallons per minute at 10 feet of head can deliver about 83 watts of useful power. Engaging the services of a hydrologist or an engineer experienced in micro-hydro systems can provide valuable insights. They can help you calculate the potential energy output and determine the best location for your intake and turbine. Furthermore, they can assist in navigating the permits and regulations governing water rights and the alteration of stream flows.

Maintenance of Hydroelectric Systems

Maintaining a micro-hydro system is mostly about vigilance and preventative care. Regular inspections ensure that each component is functioning properly and that the water flow remains consistent and free of debris. Here are some maintenance tasks to keep your system running smoothly:

- Intake Cleaning: Remove leaves, twigs, and other debris that might clog the intake screen.
- Penstock Checks: Inspect for leaks or signs of wear, especially after extreme weather events.
- Turbine and Generator Servicing: Lubricate bearings and check for any unusual noises or vibrations that could indicate wear.
- Electrical Connections: Tighten any loose connections and look for corrosion or damage to the wiring.
- Environmental Monitoring: Keep an eye on the stream's health and the impact of your system on local wildlife.

A well-maintained micro-hydro system can last for decades, providing a sustainable and eco-friendly source of power to your homestead. The investment in time and upkeep is minimal compared to the benefits of generating your own electricity from the natural flow of water on your property. With each rotation of the turbine, you're reminded of the synergy between the natural world and the ingenuity of human innovation—a synergy that powers your life in more ways than one.

Potential of Biomass Energy

Energy is all around us, not just in the wind or the flow of a river, but also in the very substance of life itself. Biomass energy is the unsung hero of renewable resources, a chameleon in the world of sustainable power. It's the organic material, both living and recently deceased, that stores sunlight in the form of chemical energy. From the leaves layering your forest floor to the food scraps decomposing in your compost, these materials are a bank of energy, ready for withdrawal with the right methods.

Understanding Biomass Energy Conversion

At its heart, biomass energy conversion is a process of release. It's a liberating of the energy bound within biological materials through combustion, biological digestion, or conversion to gas or liquid fuels. Think of it as unlocking the sun's power trapped in plant fibers and waste products. When you burn wood in a stove, you're releasing the sun's warmth back into the world. But combustion is just the beginning.

Technological strides have introduced more sophisticated methods, such as anaerobic digestion, which breaks down organic matter in the absence of oxygen to produce biogas. This gas can fuel engines or heat homes, transforming yesterday's farm waste into today's energy solution. Then there's gasification, a process that subject's biomass to high temperatures and limited oxygen, creating a gas mixture that can be used for electricity or as a building block for liquid fuels.

Types of Biomass for Energy Production

The beauty of biomass lies in its diversity. Almost any organic material can be a contender for energy production. Here's a glimpse at the array of biomass resources ripe for conversion:

- **Agricultural Residues:** After the harvest, what's left in the field can be gathered. Corn stalks, wheat straw, and other crop leftovers are more than just waste; they're potential fuel.
- **Wood and Wood Waste:** Fallen branches, pruned limbs, and even sawdust from your woodshop are valuable energy sources.
- **Animal Manure and Waste:** From the cow paddock to the chicken coop, the waste produced by livestock can be a gold mine for energy production when processed correctly.

- **Food Waste:** Your kitchen scraps, outdated groceries, and even the byproducts from food processing facilities can be broken down and converted into energy.
- **Energy Crops:** Some plants are grown specifically for energy production, like fast-growing trees or grasses that can be harvested multiple times per year.

The choice of biomass for energy production can be tailored to what's locally available, reducing transportation costs and making use of resources that might otherwise go to waste. It's a circular economy, where the end of one cycle fuels the beginning of another, creating a loop of sustainability that benefits both your homestead and the environment.

Biomass Energy Storage and Usage

Storing energy from biomass is about transforming it into a form that's stable and convenient. Wood can be stacked and dried, manure can be composted, and biogas can be compressed or stored in tanks. It's a way of banking energy for future use, ensuring a steady supply even when the raw materials are not actively being produced.

When it comes to usage, biomass energy can be as versatile as the forms it takes. Wood and pellets feed stoves and boilers, providing heat through the coldest winters. Biomass can power generators, giving life to tools and appliances. Liquid biofuels pour into the tanks of vehicles, turning the residue of last year's crop into this year's transportation.

The integration of biomass into your homestead's energy system can be a game-changer. It can stand alone, providing all the power you need, or it can work in concert with other renewable sources, filling in the gaps when the sun doesn't shine or the wind doesn't blow. It's about creating a resilient, adaptable approach to energy that's tailored to the rhythm of your life and the beat of the natural world.

As you ponder the potential of biomass for your homestead, consider the full circle of life it represents. The plants that grew in the sun's light return their stored energy to you, ensuring that nothing is wasted and everything is valued. It's a testament to the enduring cycle of growth, decay, and rebirth—a cycle that you can harness for a sustainable, energy-rich future.

Living Off-Grid: Homesteading 101

Picking Your Power Source

Tailoring Energy to Fit Your Homestead

With the canvas of your land spread out before you, a palette of renewable energy options at your fingertips, it's time to paint your masterpiece of self-sufficiency. The brush strokes of solar arrays, the hues of wind turbines, the textures of flowing streams, and the depth of biomass all contribute to the energy portrait of your homestead. But the question looms—what mix of these elements will bring your vision to life? The answer lies in a keen understanding of your energy needs and a careful comparison of each power source's strengths.

Evaluating Your Homestead's Energy Profile

Begin by sketching the outlines of your daily power usage. How much electricity do you consume in a day, a month, a year? Map out the ebb and flow of your energy demands, noting the peaks of usage during high-demand seasons or times of day. Does your homestead business necessitate a consistent power supply, or do your energy needs swell and recede like the tide?

Inventory your appliances, tools, and systems that draw power. Consider not just their wattage but their hours of operation. Factor in future aspirations that may increase your energy appetite. Will the addition of a greenhouse or workshop add a significant draw? Will the installation of an electric vehicle charging station be in the cards? With this energy profile in hand, you're ready to match your needs with the appropriate renewable solutions.

Sizing Up Renewable Energy Contenders

With a clear view of your energy landscape, weigh the merits and constraints of each renewable power source. Solar energy, with its broad adaptability, might be the sunlit path for many. Yet, if your land is kissed by constant winds, turbines could be the stalwarts of your energy supply. Micro-hydro power thrives where water flows abundantly, a non-stop performer in the renewable ensemble. And biomass, with its organic versatility, can complement these sources, especially in the colder months when heating demands rise.

Each energy source brings to the table its unique rhythm:

- Solar panels excel in sun-rich locales but take a rest once the sun has set unless paired with battery storage.

- Wind turbines demand careful placement and are only dependent on appropriate wind speeds, day or night.
- Micro-hydro systems are reliable as long as water flow is consistent and is not dependent upon the sun.
- Biomass system are dependable and can use numerous sources such as wood and crop residues to manure and food waste, serving as a base load or backup in a well-rounded energy strategy.

Crafting an Energy Ensemble for Peak Performance

The secret to unlocking the full potential of renewable resources is harmonizing them into a seamless ensemble. This integrated approach, often termed a hybrid energy system, permits each source to shine while compensating for the others' downtime. For example, solar and wind power might dominate the score during the day and in gusty weather, while biomass and hydro generate additional alternative energy at night or during calm spells.

Imagine a day in the life of such a well-balanced system:

- Morning light cascades onto solar panels, waking them to generate the day's first kilowatts.
- As the day unfolds, a rising wind joins in, allowing turbines to contribute their share, offsetting the solar lull if clouds drift by.
- Come evening, as the sun sets and winds quiet, the steady hum of micro-hydro or the stored energy in biomass carries the tune through the night.

This approach not only maximizes energy yield but also weaves a safety net, ensuring that if one source falters, others can fill the void. Moreover, energy storage systems, like batteries or thermal storage, act as reservoirs, capturing excess production for use when needed. Smart controllers orchestrate this flow, channeling energy to where it's needed and ensuring none goes to waste.

Painting the full picture of your homestead's energy needs requires both a detailed brush and broad strokes. It calls for an intimate understanding of each power source and the camaraderie they can create when conducted together. With your canvas primed and your palette chosen, you stand ready to create a living masterpiece of sustainable energy that not only powers your homestead but also enriches the land it graces. With each choice and every installation, you weave a stronger thread into the fabric of a future where living off the land includes the energy that flows through it, as natural and essential as the air we breathe and the water we drink.

As the sun dips below the horizon, casting long shadows over a day well spent, you can rest assured that the energy needs of today and tomorrow are secured, nestled within the embrace of the earth and the ceaseless dance of the elements. Now, with your homestead humming with the electricity of life and nature, let us turn our attention to the precious resource that is water—its capture, its essence, and its vital role in the sustainable homestead.

References:

Advantages and Challenges of Wind Energy - https://www.energy.gov/eere/wind/advantages-and-challenges-wind-energy

Micro-Hydro Power: A Beginners Guide to Design & Beginners - https://attra.ncat.org/publication/micro-hydro-power-a-beginners-guide-to-design-and-installation/

Micro-Hydro Power: Is it Right for My Farm? - https://attra.ncat.org/publication/micro-hydro-power-is-it-right-for-my-farm/

Energy Production from Biomass - https://faculty.washington.edu/stevehar/Biomass-Overview.pdf

Comparative Analysis of Different Renewable Energy - https://www.linkedin.com/pulse/comparative-analysis-different-renewable-energy-sources-mendonza

Relevant Resources:

Homestead.org: Alternative Energy- https://www.homestead.org/alternative-energy/living-without-an-electric-bill/

OffGridPermaculture.com: Off Grid Hydro-Electric & Micro -Hydro How-To Guide- https://offgridpermaculture.com/Off_Grid_Energy/Off_Grid_Hyrdo_Electric__Micro_Hydro_How_To_Guide.html

Energy.gov: Planning a Micro-Hydropower System - https://www.energy.gov/energysaver/planning-microhydropower-system

Alternative Energy Tutorials: Wind Turbine Design for Wind Power - https://www.alternative-energy-tutorials.com/wind-energy/wind-turbine-design.html

Missouri Wind & Solar: https://windandsolar.com

Energypedia: Small Scale Electricity Generation from Biomass - https://energypedia.info/images/9/93/Small-Scale_Electricity_Generation_From_Biomass_Part-1.pdf

Diagram of a Rainwater Collection System by WaterCache.com

Living Off-Grid: Homesteading 101

Diagram of a Rainwater Collection System by WaterCache.com

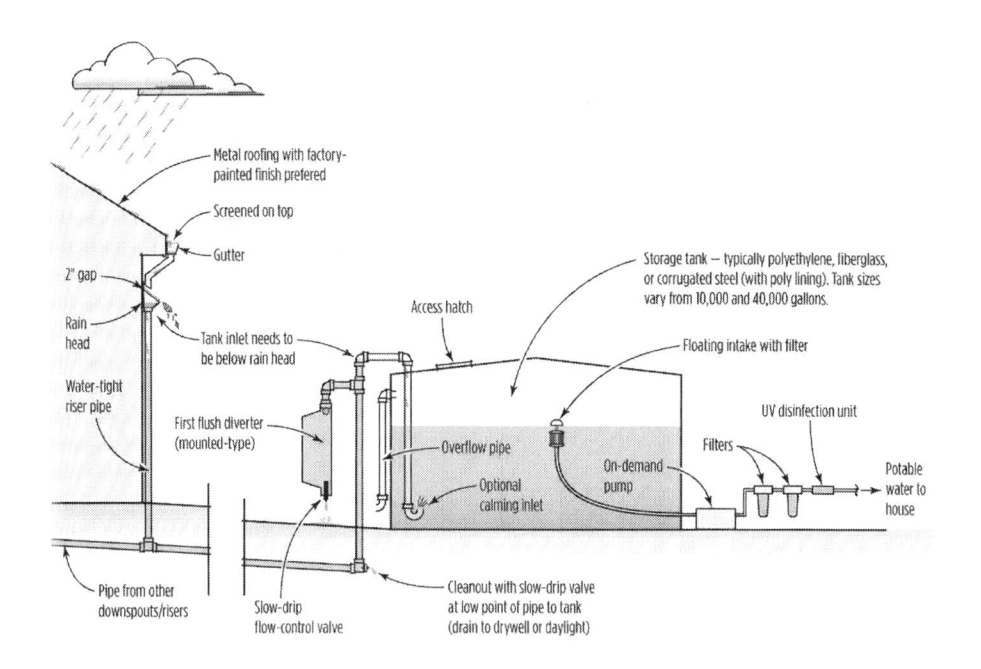

Chapter 5

Rainwater Collection and Storage

Building an Efficient Rainwater Harvesting System

Imagine each drop of rain as a potential symphony, a cascade of notes ready to be orchestrated into a resource that quenches your garden, washes your clothes, and even, with the right touch, provides a glass of water to sip on a hot summer day. Rainwater, the sky's gift, arrives unbidden and often unnoticed, slipping through our gutters and down our drains, while it could be fulfilling the needs of our homesteads. In this chapter, we will try to not let a single drop of that potential go to waste.

Rainwater harvesting is an age-old practice getting a modern makeover. It's about capturing what nature provides and channeling it into a resource you can tap on demand. But before you place your first barrel or lay a single pipe, there's groundwork to be done—literally and figuratively.

Site Assessment for Rainwater Collection

The first step in designing an efficient rainwater harvesting system is a thorough site assessment. Look up. Where does the rain fall? Your roof is prime real estate for collection, but its material, angle, and size all play a part in how much water you can catch. Consider the layout of your land and the journey water takes once it hits the ground. Are there slopes that can direct the flow? Any existing structures that can house storage tanks?

Understanding your region's rainfall patterns is crucial. In areas with sporadic, heavy downpours, your system needs to handle sudden influxes of water. Conversely, in climates with steady, gentle rains, your setup can be fine-tuned for gradual collection.

Designing a Rainwater Harvesting System

Designing your system is a balance between what you need and what nature can provide. Start with your water usage—how much do you need for irrigation, livestock, or household chores? Then, look to your roof. A simple calculation can estimate how much rainwater you can collect: multiply the square footage of your roof by the rainfall in inches and then by 0.623 to get gallons of collectible water.

Your design blueprint should include:

- **Gutters and Downspouts:** Channeling rain from roof to tank.
- **First Flush Diverters:** Ensuring the initial, dirtier water doesn't enter your storage.
- **Filters:** Keeping leaves and debris out.
- **Storage Tanks:** Where your water will be held.
- **Delivery System:** How water gets from the tank to where it's needed, which can include gravity-fed irrigation or a more complex pump-driven system.

Materials Needed for Rainwater Harvesting

Quality materials are the nuts and bolts of a lasting rainwater system. Opt for UV-resistant PVC or metal for gutters and downspouts. Ensure your tanks are made of food-grade material if you plan on using the water for drinking, and consider opaque materials to prevent algae growth. Your filters can range from simple mesh screens to more sophisticated first-flush systems that discard the first rain, which carries most of the debris.

Installation Process for Rainwater Harvesting System

Roll up your sleeves—it's time to install. Begin with gutters and downspouts, ensuring they're securely attached and angled to direct water toward your storage tanks. Install your first flush system and filters, and then set your storage tanks on a solid, level base, preferably raised to assist with gravity-fed distribution.

Remember, water is heavy. A gallon weighs over 8.34 pounds, so a full tank is a force to reckon with. Secure your tanks in place and double-check all connections for leaks. For those using pumps, follow the manufacturer's instructions carefully, and make sure your electrical connections are safe and dry.

Maintenance of Rainwater Harvesting System

Just like a garden, your rainwater system thrives with regular care. Clean gutters and filters seasonally and inspect your tanks for cracks or leaks. Keep an eye on your first flush diverters and empty them after each significant rain. Monitoring your system not only keeps it running efficiently but also helps you understand its rhythm and nuances, informing you when it's ready for use and when it needs a little TLC.

Your rainwater harvesting system is more than a utility; it's a statement of sustainability, a commitment to working with the environment, and a step toward resilience. It's about recognizing the worth in every drop of rain and giving it purpose—a purpose that sustains your homestead and respects the cycles of nature. With your system in place, you can sit back and listen to the rain with a new appreciation, knowing that you're capturing a resource as old as time and as fresh as the sky above.

Storage Solutions for Rainwater

Crafting the perfect rainwater storage solution is similar to choosing the ideal container for your homegrown harvest. The options are as varied as they are functional, each with unique benefits tailored to your homestead's layout and your personal water usage needs. In this section, we'll explore the different vessels that can hold your collected rainwater, keeping it safe and sound for when you need it most.

Above Ground Rainwater Storage Tanks

Elevating your water storage with above-ground tanks is like adding a watchtower to your homestead—it's visible, accessible, and stands as a testament to your commitment to sustainability. These tanks come in an array of sizes and materials, including polyethylene, metal, or fiberglass, all durable choices designed to withstand the elements. Positioning is key for these tanks; a spot with ample sunlight will ward off the chill during colder months, helping to prevent freezing, while shade in the summer will keep the water cool and algae at bay.

One significant advantage of above-ground tanks is the ease of installation. They require no excavation, just a solid, level foundation to sit upon. Monitoring levels and performing maintenance becomes a straightforward task, with everything within arm's reach. When it comes to distribution, gravity does the heavy lifting, sending water cascading through your system with the turn of a valve.

Underground Rainwater Storage Tanks

Buried beneath your homestead's surface, underground rainwater storage tanks offer a discreet alternative to their above-ground counterparts. They're the secret cellars of water storage, kept out of sight and mind, preserving the aesthetic of your land. These subterranean tanks capitalize on the insulating properties of the earth, maintaining a consistent temperature that protects against freezing and limits algae growth.

The installation of underground tanks is an excavation endeavor, requiring careful planning and a touch of engineering. Once nestled in the ground, they're often outlasted by the landscape, with only their access points peeking out. Pumps become the lifeline for your water, drawing it from the depths to where it's needed. While they come with the additional cost and complexity of pumping systems, the trade-off is a lower impact on the landscape and protection from the wear and tear of weather.

Rain Barrels for Small-Scale Storage

For those just dipping their toes into rainwater collection or homesteaders with modest water requirements, rain barrels are the quintessential starting point. These barrels, often repurposed from food storage or transport, are the foot soldiers of rainwater storage, easily deployed wherever they're needed. They nestle against the house, beneath downspouts, ready to catch whatever the skies offer.

Rain barrels exemplify simplicity. They don't demand elaborate setups; a secure stand to elevate them for gravity-fed watering, a screen to keep out debris and mosquitoes, and a spigot from which to draw water are all the essentials required. Their small footprint and ease of use make rain barrels ideal for garden irrigation or outdoor washing tasks.

Maintenance of Rainwater Storage Solutions

The stewardship of your rainwater storage solutions is a year-round commitment, ensuring every drop is ready for use when called upon. Regular inspections of tanks, whether above or below ground, prevent surprises, allowing you to spot issues before they escalate. Checking for algae growth, sediment buildup, and signs of wear and tear like cracks or seal degradation is key.

For above-ground tanks, a seasonal cleaning ritual keeps the water clear and the tanks functioning well. Scrubbing away any algae, flushing out sediment, and ensuring overflows are clear and free of blockages primes your system for peak performance. Underground tanks require less frequent but more thorough inspections, often involving a professional to ensure the integrity of the tank is unimpaired.

Rain barrels, with their more accessible nature, benefit from a routine rinse and refresh. As the seasons change, so does the care they require—emptying and storing them during freezing weather prevents cracking, while a thorough cleaning before the rainy season preps them for the influx of fresh water.

Each storage solution, with its own set of maintenance rituals, plays an integral role in the seamless operation of your rainwater harvesting system. Whether you're relying on the robust capacity of a large tank or the convenience of a rain barrel, the care you invest ensures a bounty of rainwater is always within reach, ready to sustain your homestead's diverse needs.

Ensuring Water Quality

Regular Testing of Rainwater Quality

The quality of your collected rainwater is more than a detail—it's the linchpin that determines its suitability for varying uses, from irrigation to personal consumption. Initiating a regimen of water testing is not merely proactive; it's a necessary step in ensuring the health and safety of your homestead. This begins with understanding what you're testing for: pH levels, contaminants, and pathogens that could impact water quality.

Setting up a schedule for periodic water testing is much like marking the seasons. You might test more frequently during the first flush of spring or after a particularly dusty dry spell. Testing kits are readily available at local hardware stores and online, providing the tools to measure a range of potential issues, from mineral content to bacterial presence. For more in-depth analysis, sending samples to a certified lab offers a detailed profile of your water's characteristics.

Filtration Systems for Rainwater

Integrating a filtration system into your rainwater setup is an investment in clarity and purity. It transforms your collected rainwater from a raw asset into a refined resource. Filtration options are plentiful and can be tailored to the specific needs identified in your water tests. Simple mesh filters keep out larger debris, while more complex multi-stage systems tackle finer particulates, odors, and even some dissolved substances.

Activated carbon filters are a popular choice, drawing out chemicals and toxins with their porous, absorbent nature. Ceramic filters add a layer of bacterial protection, trapping pathogens as water passes through their microscopic pores. Ultraviolet light systems provide a non-chemical disinfection option, using high-intensity light to neutralize bacteria and viruses. The appropriate combination of these systems elevates your rainwater, preparing it for its intended role, whether that's watering your garden or washing your dishes.

Safe Handling and Storage Practices

The sanctity of your water is not only reliant on the initial collection and filtration but also on the practices that follow. Safe handling and storage are the guardians of water quality, maintaining the purity of your supply. This encompasses everything from using clean containers for transport to ensuring taps and access points are free from contaminants. It means protecting storage tanks from intrusion by insects or small animals and shielding water from sunlight to prevent algae growth.

Creating a protocol for anyone interacting with your water system instills a culture of cleanliness. It might include washing hands before accessing storage tanks or using dedicated hoses and pumps that are regularly cleaned and only used for potable water. This vigilance ensures that the integrity of your water is preserved from collection to tap.

Addressing Common Water Quality Issues

Even with the best-laid plans, water quality issues can arise, but knowing how to identify and rectify them keeps your system on track. Discoloration might signal the presence of tannins from organic matter or rust from corroded components, calling for a review of your filtration setup or an inspection of your system's infrastructure. A sulphuric smell can indicate bacteria, which might be resolved by "shocking the system" with a concentrated chlorine treatment or the introduction of an ultraviolet purification step.

Turbidity, or cloudiness, in your water, could be due to fine sediments slipping through your filtration system. A sediment filter with a finer micron rating might be required. If water tests reveal a high concentration of heavy metals treating the water may include specialized filters or chemicals that bind and remove these contaminants.

Adjusting your system to address these issues is a continuous process, the result of a dialogue between your observations and the water's performance. Develop a relationship with your local Co-op and other local homesteaders in the area, as they may be experiencing the same issues. It requires attention to subtle shifts in quality and a willingness to adapt and fine-tune. With a commitment to ongoing testing and a responsive approach to filtration and handling, your rainwater becomes a trusted, vital component of your homestead's lifeblood, as pure as the intentions behind its collection.

Legal Aspects of Rainwater Collection

Understanding Local Laws and Regulations

Diving into the world of rainwater collection you must first navigate the intricate web of local laws and regulations. These rules form the backbone of environmental stewardship and public health in your community. They vary widely from one jurisdiction to another, reflecting the unique climates, water needs, and legal philosophies of different regions.

In some areas, rainwater collection is encouraged, seen as a means to reduce demand on municipal systems and promote conservation. Other localities may place restrictions on the practice, often due to historical water rights laws where water is a carefully allocated resource. Familiarizing yourself with these local laws not only keeps you compliant but also informs you of potential incentives that may support your rainwater harvesting endeavors.

Obtaining Necessary Permits and Licenses

The next step often involves securing permits or licenses, a process that might seem daunting but serves to align your system with safety standards and environmental guidelines. This is where due diligence pays dividends. Contacting your local building department or environmental agency is your starting point. They can provide information on the specific permits required, whether for construction, plumbing, or environmental impact.

The permit process typically involves submitting plans for your system and may include inspections to ensure that your setup meets the necessary criteria. This phase is not merely a bureaucratic hoop to jump through; it's a safeguard for you and your community, ensuring that your rainwater collection system is both effective and safe.

Navigating Building Codes and Standards

Building codes and standards are the rulebooks of construction, community, and safety. They ensure that systems are built to last and perform as intended. When it comes to rainwater harvesting, these codes can dictate everything from the materials you use to the methods of installation, and continued maintenance.

Adhering to these standards often means working closely with professionals who are well-versed in the legal and practical aspects of rainwater system design. They can help you navigate the fine print and ensure that your system not only meets the local building codes but also operates at peak efficiency. In doing so, you safeguard not just your own homestead but also the broader ecosystem it inhabits.

Advocacy for Rainwater Collection Rights

In regions where rainwater collection faces legal limitations, advocacy becomes a tool for change. Joining forces with like-minded individuals and groups can lead to a reevaluation of outdated regulations. Communities often evolve, and laws can too. Advocacy involves education, outreach, and sometimes, a push for legislative change.

Support can come from environmental groups, agricultural organizations, or even local government bodies that recognize the benefits of rainwater collection in sustainable living and resource conservation. By adding your voice to the chorus calling for the responsible legalization and regulation of rainwater harvesting, you help to pave the way for future generations of eco-conscious citizens.

With a clear understanding of the legal landscape and a commitment to navigating it thoughtfully, your rainwater harvesting efforts become part of a larger movement towards sustainability. It's a movement that respects the delicate balance of our ecosystems and acknowledges the role that each individual plays in preserving our planet's most precious resources.

As we close this chapter on the intricacies of rainwater collection, we carry with us the knowledge that every drop saved is a stride towards a more resilient and self-sufficient homestead. Collecting rainwater is more than a practical endeavor; it is a profound connection to the natural world, a partnership with the sky above that nourishes the earth below. With our systems in place and the legal framework navigated, we stand ready to embrace the rain, each storm cloud on the horizon a promise of sustenance and sustainability for the days to come.

References:

Design of Rainwater Harvesting Systems in Oklahoma - https://extension.okstate.edu/fact-sheets/design-of-rainwater-harvesting-systems-in-oklahoma.html

National Tank Outlet: Plastic vs Steel Rainwater Harvesting Tanks - https://www.ntotank.com/blog/plastic-vs-steel-rainwater-tanks

Rainwater Harvesting Regulations Map - https://www.energy.gov/femp/rainwater-harvesting-regulations-map

Exploring the Link Between Rainwater Harvesting and Improved Water Quality Standards - https://utilitiesone.com/rainwater-harvesting-and-water-quality-ensuring-safe-and-clean-water-supplies

Relevant Resources:

How to Design a Rainwater Harvesting System - https://www.liveabout.com/design-a-rainwater-harvesting-system-in-6-steps-3157815

Rainwater Harvesting Systems Technology Review - https://www.energy.gov/femp/rainwater-harvesting-systems-technology-review

Rainwater Collection and Storage

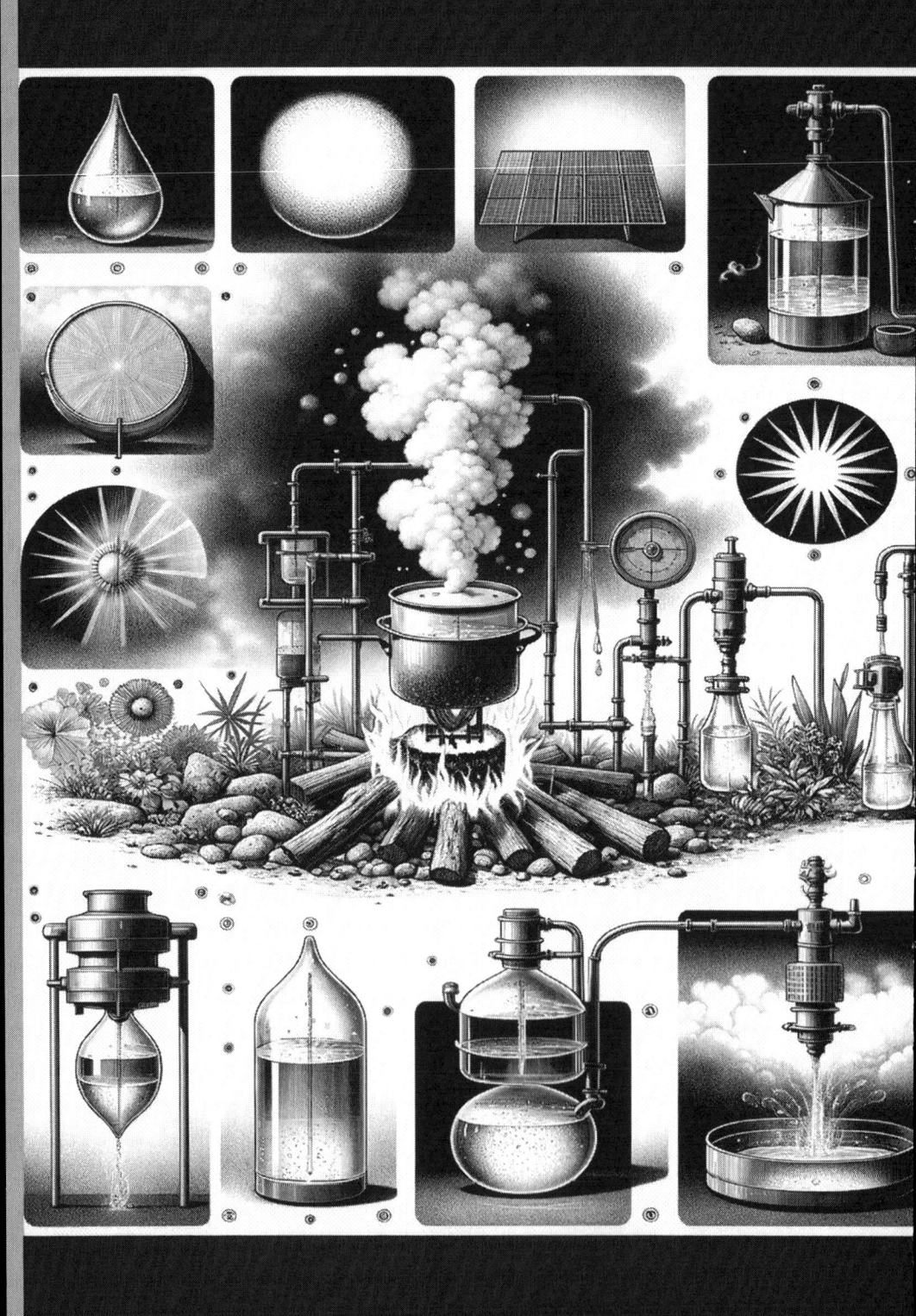

Chapter 6
Navigating Water Purification

Water, the sustainer of life and the most unassuming of daily necessities, can be as deceptive as a mirage in the desert. It flows from our taps and fills our glasses with an appearance of crystal clarity yet hidden within its transparent depths can lurk unseen dangers. This life-giving substance we so often take for granted requires our vigilance to ensure its purity. For the homesteader, understanding the nuances of water purification is less about luxury and more about safeguarding the very essence of our well-being.

In the realm of rainwater collection and natural water sources, the distinction between clear and clean water is paramount. While the former is pleasing to the eye, the latter is crucial for health. It's not just about aesthetics; it's about biology, chemistry, and a bit of elbow grease. So, let's roll up our sleeves and wade into the waters of purification, where vigilance meets action in the quest for safe hydration.

Health Risks of Contaminated Water

Water's journey from cloud to cup is fraught with potential for contamination. As it kisses the earth, it can pick up unwanted passengers—microbes that can turn a refreshing drink into a health hazard. Pathogens like E. coli, Giardia, and Cryptosporidium are notorious for gatecrashing the water supply party, bringing with them symptoms that no one invited: gastrointestinal distress, fever, and worse.

Chemical contaminants also pose a threat. They're the silent types, often undetectable without testing. Pesticides, heavy metals, and even residues from airborne pollutants can seep into water sources, building up in our systems over time and potentially leading to chronic health issues.

Common Contaminants in Rainwater

Rainwater, while a gift from the skies, is not exempt from contamination. As it cascades over rooftops, it can collect anything lying in wait—bird droppings, dead insects, or leaves decomposing into a microbial playground. Even the materials from which we construct our collection systems can contribute to contamination, leaching chemicals into the water we intend to use for our gardens, our livestock, and ourselves.

Take, for example, a simple setup with gutters and a storage barrel. That barrel, unless properly covered and filtered, can become a breeding ground for bacteria, a repository for debris, or a chemical mixer if not made of the right materials. The purity of rainwater is not a given; it is a goal that requires intention and action to achieve.

Importance of Regular Water Testing

Testing your water is not just a precaution; it's an act of empowerment. Knowing what's in your water is the first step toward ensuring its safety. It's the same principle as knowing the soil composition of your garden beds—you can't amend and improve what you haven't measured.

Many organizations, such as local environmental agencies, water conservation groups, or agricultural extension offices, might offer free or low-cost rainwater testing kits or can direct you to resources that do. Try contacting local environmental protection agencies, universities with environmental science departments, or your local co-op for specific information on rainwater testing in your area.

Regular water testing provides a snapshot of your water's health. It alerts you to changes in quality that might necessitate a change in purification strategy or signal an issue with your collection system. Test for bacteria, pH levels, and chemical contaminants. Local extension offices or environmental agencies often offer testing kits or services, giving you the tools to keep a close eye on your water's condition. If you need help or have any questions, you will find these people very knowledgeable, helpful and more than willing to share their experiences.

Maintaining a log to record testing results is recommended to see the history of your testing results which may show seasonal trends in the quality of your rainwater. You will have this logbook for some time, so it should be durable, and have a waterproof cover. Inside you should maintain columns indicating 1) the date and time of the test, 2) the type of test, 3) where you obtained the test kit, 4) the test results, and 5) action taken, as well as 6) any notes regarding testing conditions that might be important.

Types of Tests for Rainwater Testing

Bacterial Testing. Purpose is to determine if E. coli, Cryptosporidium, Giardia, or other coliforms are in the water. Coliforms indicate that the water is contaminated by fecal matter which can cause food poisoning and can make people very sick.

pH Testing. Results range between 0 [acidic] to 14 [basic] where the preferred pH levels range between 6.5 to 8.5. If your water is too acidic your water may be corrosive. If your water is too basic, digestive issues like nausea, vomiting and stomach pain may occur.

Alkalinity Testing. Measures the capacity of water to neutralize acids, or to resist acidic changes in pH.

Chemical Contamination Testing. Detecting the presence of heavy metals such as mercury, arsenic, and pesticides.

By testing your water on a regular basis until you are satisfied that you understand the nature of the rainwater in your area you are insuring the following:

- **Health Protection:** Identifying harmful contaminants can prevent illness and health complications.
- **System Maintenance:** Testing can reveal issues in your collection or storage systems that need attention.
- **Peace of Mind:** Knowing your water is safe can provide comfort and assurance in your homestead's sustainability.

Water purification is a multifaceted challenge, one that intertwines with the very fabric of homesteading life. It's as much about understanding the risks as it is about implementing solutions. It's a commitment to the health and well-being of your family and your land. With an informed and proactive approach, you can transform rainwater and natural sources into a safe, life-sustaining resource. Your homestead deserves nothing less than water in its purest essence—a foundation for a thriving, self-sufficient life.

DIY Water Purification Methods

Clean water is a cornerstone of a healthy homestead. While commercial water purifiers are a sound investment, there's a certain satisfaction that comes with purifying water using your own ingenuity and resources at hand. Here we explore several DIY methods that ensure every drop you consume is as pure as nature intended.

Boiling for Water Purification

The simplicity of boiling water contradicts its effectiveness. Heat serves as a universal purifier, laying waste to nearly all disease-causing organisms that may be present in your water. This method, practiced for centuries, remains a reliable standby. To properly purify water by boiling, follow these steps:

- Fill a pot with water from your collection system.
- Bring the water to a rolling boil for at least one minute, or three minutes at higher altitudes where water boils at lower temperatures.
- Allow the water to cool naturally without adding ice, as this could reintroduce contaminants.
- Store the cooled water in clean, sanitized containers with tight-fitting lids.

This method doesn't remove chemical contaminants, but it's an excellent line of defense against pathogens when other purification methods aren't available.

Solar Disinfection Technique

Harnessing the sun's ultraviolet rays, solar disinfection—or SODIS—is a technique that uses sunlight to improve water quality. Clear plastic bottles are filled with water and set in direct sunlight for a minimum of six hours on a sunny day, or two consecutive days if the weather is overcast. The UV radiation works in tandem with increased temperature to incapacitate harmful microorganisms.

Navigating Water Purification

Here's how to maximize the effectiveness of SODIS:

Choose clear, colorless plastic bottles without scratches or cloudiness.

- Fill the bottles with water, ensuring there are no air bubbles.
- Lay the bottles horizontally on a reflective surface, such as metal roofing or aluminum foil, to enhance UV exposure.
- After the required exposure time, the treated water should be consumed or transferred to clean storage containers.

Homemade Water Filters

Crafting a water filter from scratch can be a gratifying project. By layering natural materials that each play a role in filtration, you can construct a device that clarifies and partly purifies your water. A basic homemade filter might include:

- Gravel or small stones as the bottommost layer to catch larger debris.
- Sand above the gravel to trap smaller particles.
- Activated charcoal, if available, to remove some chemical contaminants and improve taste.
- A final layer of clean cloth or coffee filters at the top to screen out sediment before the water enters the filtration media.

While this setup won't remove all contaminants, it's a step towards cleaner water and can be used as a pre-treatment before boiling or disinfection.

Distillation Process for Water Purification

The distillation process is a science experiment come to life, replicating the earth's natural water cycle on a micro-scale. By boiling water and then condensing the steam back into a liquid, you can separate pure water from many of its impurities. Here's a simple way to distill water at home:

- Fill a large pot halfway with water from your collection system.
- Place a smaller pot or heat-safe container inside the larger one to catch distilled water.
- Invert the lid of the large pot so that the highest point is directly above the smaller container. The lid should be able to collect and funnel condensation.

- Bring the water to a boil and then reduce to a simmer, ensuring steam condenses on the lid and drips into the smaller container.
- Continue the process until you've collected enough distilled water, then allow it to cool before storing.

This method effectively removes a broad range of contaminants, including pathogens, heavy metals, and salts, making it ideal for purifying drinking water. However, it is energy-intensive and may not be suitable for large volumes unless you have a dedicated solar distillation setup.

Each of these DIY methods provides a different level of purification, and they can be used in combination to achieve cleaner water. Boiling is unparalleled in its ability to kill bacteria and viruses. Solar disinfection offers a passive, energy-free option, though it requires clear skies and patience. Homemade filters are excellent for a first pass to remove particulates and some chemicals, while distillation is the most thorough method, capable of producing high-purity water.

Incorporating these methods into your homestead routine can become second nature, ensuring that you have access to clean water for all your needs. Whether you're filling a pot for cooking, topping off a birdbath, or quenching your thirst after a day's work, these purification techniques stand as a testament to self-reliance and the ingenuity that defines the homesteading spirit.

Purchasing and Maintaining Water Purifiers

Choosing the Right Water Purifier for Your Needs

Embarking on the quest for the perfect water purifier is no small task. It calls for a keen evaluation of your household's water usage, the specific impurities you need to address, and the flow rate that will keep up with your demand. A family's daily activities, from preparing meals to showering, dictate the capacity and type of purifier required. For instance, a high-capacity reverse osmosis system might be the answer for a household aiming to reduce a wide spectrum of contaminants, including fluoride and dissolved salts. Alternatively, for those focusing solely on biological contaminants, an ultraviolet light purifier could be the ideal choice.

The selection process involves comparing the effectiveness of various models against your list of known water impurities – which should be identified through previous testing. Look for certifications that guarantee the removal of specific contaminants. The size and installation location of the unit also weigh heavily in the decision-making process. Some systems fit snugly under a sink, while others may require more dedicated space.

Consider the long-term costs as well. Beyond the initial investment, factor in the expense of replacement filters or any additional treatments the system might necessitate. The goal is to find a balance between initial outlay, ongoing maintenance costs, and the peace of mind that comes with pure, clean water.

Installation of Water Purifiers

Once you've pinpointed the purifier that aligns with your needs, installing it correctly is vital for optimum performance. Many systems come with detailed instructions suited for a DIY installation, while others might require professional assistance, especially if they integrate into your home's plumbing. Ensuring that the system is accessible for future maintenance is paramount, so plan the location with foresight.

For countertop models or those that attach directly to a faucet, setup typically involves basic steps such as connecting hoses or adaptors. More complex systems, like under-sink or whole-house purifiers, might necessitate turning off the water supply, drilling to accommodate new faucets, and configuring connections to existing pipes. Following the manufacturer's guidelines closely during installation not only ensures the system functions as it should but also safeguards your warranty.

Routine Maintenance of Water Purifiers

After installation, your water purifier will require regular check-ups to maintain its purifying prowess. Each model has its own maintenance schedule, which usually involves changing filters at prescribed intervals. Some systems have indicators that alert you when it's time for a filter change, while others rely on a set schedule. Staying on top of these changes is crucial; a filter past its prime is a liability, potentially allowing contaminants to pass through or, worse, becoming a breeding ground for bacteria.

Cleaning the system is also part of routine upkeep. Certain models may require periodic descaling, especially in areas with hard water, to prevent mineral buildup that can hamper efficiency. Consult the owner's manual for specific instructions on cleaning and maintaining your system to ensure lasting effectiveness and prevent issues down the line.

Troubleshooting Common Water Purifier Issues

Even with meticulous maintenance, water purifiers can sometimes encounter issues. A decrease in water flow could indicate a clogged filter or a problem with the supply line. If the water starts to taste off or if there's a sudden change in its quality, it's time to investigate—begin with the most recent filter change and work back from there.

Should your system suddenly stop working, first check for any obvious signs of mechanical failure, such as leaks or loose connections. Next, review the power supply to electronic components like UV lamps or pumps. If the system uses a battery, ensure it's charged or replace it if necessary.

For more complex issues, such as persistent low pressure or unusual noises, refer to the troubleshooting section of your manual or seek support from the manufacturer. Keeping a log of maintenance and any issues encountered not only helps diagnose problems but also provides a record that can be helpful for warranty support or professional repairs.

The act of selecting, installing, and maintaining a water purifier is one of the many threads that weave the fabric of a self-reliant homestead. It's a commitment to the health and comfort of your family, an investment in the longevity of your self-sustaining lifestyle. With the right system in place, tended to with care, the water that sustains your homestead will continue to flow pure and clean, a testament to the diligence and foresight at the heart of homesteading.

Water Purification in Emergency Situations

In the throes of an emergency, when the usual comforts of modern infrastructure are stripped away, the ability to access clean water becomes critical. Whether due to natural disasters, power outages, or unforeseen events, having a plan for purifying water can mean the difference between resilience and vulnerability. Here, we explore practical strategies for securing safe water when circumstances are unpredictable and conventional methods may not be available.

Quick and Effective Emergency Purification Techniques

In times of urgency, speed and simplicity are your allies. Certain techniques can be implemented swiftly with minimal equipment. Iodine tablets, for instance, are small but mighty tools that can disinfect a liter of water typically within 30 minutes. Similarly, chlorine bleach, a staple in many households, can be used in small amounts to treat large quantities of water, making it safe for consumption. Just a few drops per gallon, and after a 30-minute wait, the water is typically ready to drink. It's important, however, to use unscented bleach that's intended for disinfection and to follow the recommended guidelines to avoid incorrect dosages.

Another fast-acting solution is the use of a portable, hand-pumped water filter. These devices are designed to move water through filtration media quickly, efficiently removing pathogens and particulates. With a hand pump, even murky water from a river or a pond can be transformed into drinkable water in mere moments.

Portable Water Purifiers for Emergency Use

Portable water purifiers are indispensable in your emergency toolkit. These compact devices come in various forms, from straw filters that cleanse water as you drink, to pump filters that can process larger volumes for cooking or medical use. Gravity-fed bags that filter water as it flows from a higher to a lower point are another option, requiring no effort other than the initial setup.

When selecting portable purifiers, look for ones that remove viruses, bacteria, and protozoa. Durability is also essential—your device should be able to withstand the rigors of an emergency situation. Ensure you're familiar with its operation before an emergency arises; in a high-stress scenario, you'll want to use your purifier confidently and efficiently.

Stockpiling Purification Supplies

A prepared homesteader is one who thinks ahead, and stockpiling purification supplies is a proactive step towards self-reliance. Your storage should include a variety of items to ensure you have multiple ways to treat water. Include iodine tablets, chlorine bleach, and sediment filters. Add to this a supply of coffee filters or cloth for pre-filtering to extend the life of your purification tools.

It's also wise to have replacement parts for any mechanical purifiers you might use, such as extra O-rings, seals, and filters. Keep these supplies in a designated area, clearly labeled and easily accessible. Rotate your stock to ensure nothing expires or deteriorates, keeping your emergency water purification supplies in prime condition.

Emergency Water Storage Tips

In addition to purification, proper storage of water is central to emergency preparedness. Ideally, you'll have a reserve of treated water ready for use. Store this water in clean, food-grade containers away from direct sunlight and temperature extremes. Large barrels or dedicated water storage tanks with spigots can provide a substantial supply, while smaller containers offer portability if you need to relocate.

Consider the amount of water you'll need: a minimum of one gallon per person per day is a common recommendation, with additional allowances for cooking, cleaning, and any medical needs. Regularly rotate your stored water, using and replenishing your supply to keep it fresh. In freezing climates, leave space in your containers for expansion to prevent cracking.

With these emergency water purification and storage strategies in hand, you fortify your homestead against the unexpected. You create a buffer against the unpredictability of nature and the frailties of man-made systems. Preparedness is not a reaction; it's a way of life that values foresight and readiness, ensuring that come what may, the wellspring of life in the form of clean, drinkable water remains within your grasp.

In the next chapter, we will cast our eyes toward the soil beneath our feet, exploring the art of cultivation and the cycles of growth that sustain us. From the tiniest seed to the mightiest tree, the earth offers up its bounty, and we, as stewards of the land, are tasked with nurturing and harvesting its abundance.

References:

A Global Review of the Microbiological Quality and Potential Health Risks Associated with Roof Harvested Rainwater Tanks - https://www.nature.com/articles/s41545-019-0030-5

DIY Water Filtration Methods - https://energy5.com/blog/diy-water-filtration-methods

ThePrepared.com: Best Home Water Filter - https://theprepared.com/homestead/reviews/home-water-filter/

Centers for Disease Control and Prevention: Control and Prevention: Choosing Home Water Filters & Other Water Treatment Systems - https://www.cdc.gov/healthywater/drinking/home-water-treatment/water-filters/step1.html

Making Water Safe in an Emergency - https://www.cdc.gov/healthywater/emergency/making-water-safe.html

Relevant Resources:

ProOne vs Berkey Filters: Ultimate Guide to Best Water Purity - https://waterfilterdirect.com/blogs/industry-articles/proone-vs-berkey-the-ultimate-showdown-of-water-filtration-systems

Pioneer Water Tanks: Choose Your Water Tank - https://pioneerwatertanksamerica.com/choose-your-water-tank/

Gravity Fed Water Systems: A Simple Overview - https://homesteading.com/gravity-fed-water-systems-overview/

American Rainwater Catchment Systems Association - https://www.arcsa.org/

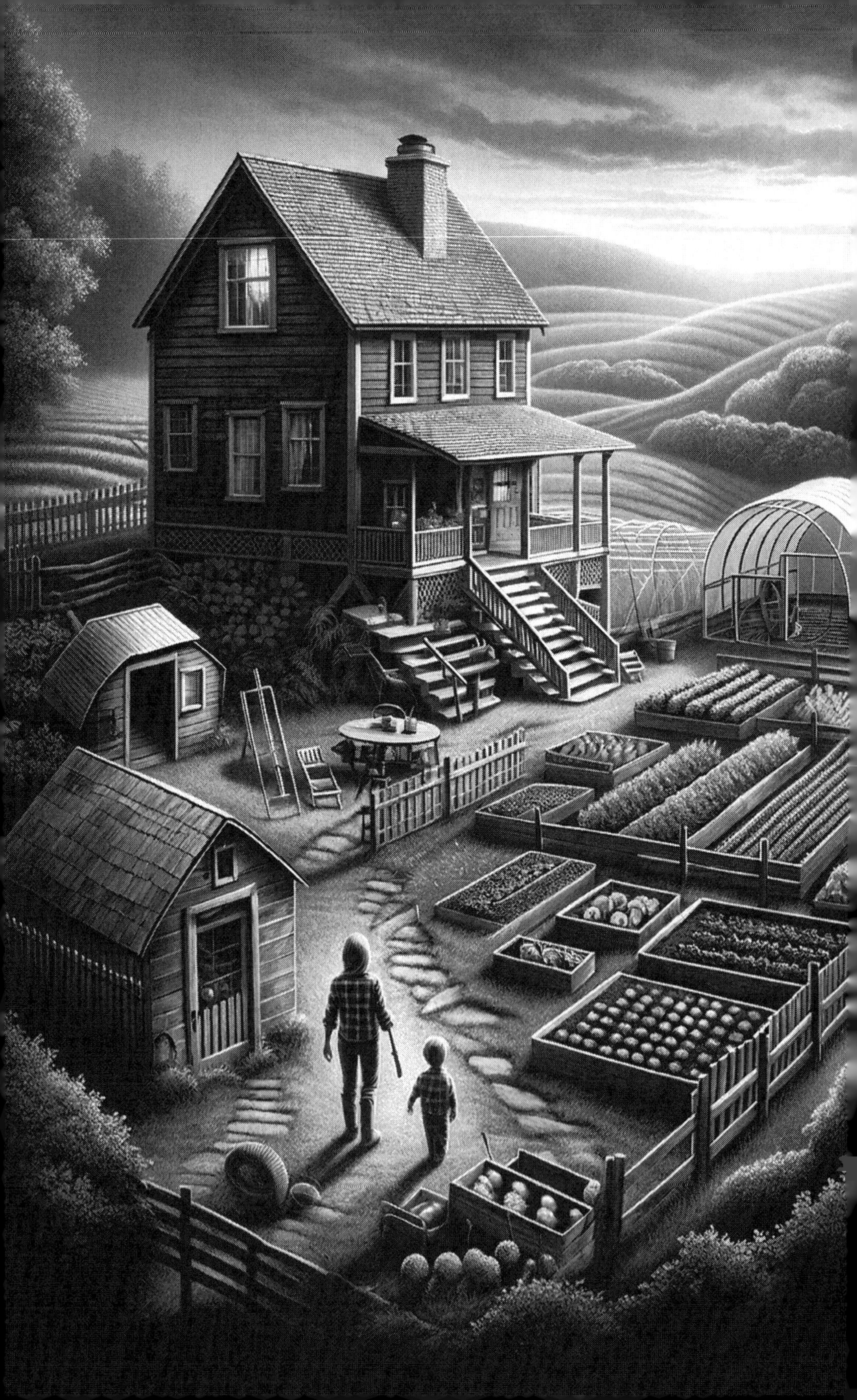

Chapter 7
Year-Round Food Production

Your Homestead Garden

Imagine your homestead as a blank canvas, the soil beneath your feet waiting for the brushstrokes of your labor to transform it into a vibrant tapestry of greens, yellows, and reds. Your garden is not just a plot of land; it is a living, breathing ecosystem that thrives under your careful watch. It's the bedrock of your self-sufficiency, a tangible expression of your dedication to the land. Here, in the sacred dance between human and earth, a well-planned garden becomes the heartbeat of the homestead.

Now, forget the notion of haphazardly tossing seeds to the wind and hoping for the best. Gardening on your homestead is a deliberate act, a strategic game of chess played with Mother Nature as your partner. It's about making informed decisions, understanding the lay of the land, and timing your moves with the seasons. Let's roll up our sleeves and get our hands dirty as we lay the groundwork for a garden that yields a bounty fit for the kings and queens of homesteading.

Planning Your Homestead Garden

Site Selection - Vegetables Don't Like Wet Feet

Selecting the perfect spot for your garden is a bit like choosing a home—it needs to be just right. You want a location that catches the sun's early rays and

Living Off-Grid: Homesteading 101

basks in its warmth throughout the day. Observe your property at different times for every season to see where and how the sun arcs from season to season. It is quite amazing to see how much the shade moves from summer to winter solstice.

Consider the lay of the land—slight slopes are good for drainage, but avoid areas where water pools after a rain, unless you plan on growing rice or watercress. For a vegetable garden with moist soil, but not necessarily soggy, consider these vegetables: celery, lettuce, spinach, cabbage, swiss chard and peas.

Also, try to have your water source close to your garden, in order to reduce the labor of watering. And don't forget about wind patterns; a spot sheltered from harsh winds will protect delicate plants and the dehydration the wind can cause.

Soil Testing

Your soil is the foundation of your garden, and just like you wouldn't build a house on shaky ground, you shouldn't plant without knowing what's below the surface. Soil testing reveals its secrets—the pH levels, nutrient content, and composition. Home testing kits are readily available, or you can send a sample to a local extension service for a more detailed analysis. Just like the rainwater testing logbook discussed in Chapter 5, create another logbook to record soil testing, garden layout for crop rotation and seed germination results. The columns in your logbook should include date, location, pH Level, nitrogen content, phosphorus content, potassium content, amendments applied, and any other notes deemed important or interesting. With these results in hand, you'll know exactly what amendments are needed. Below is a chart of common deficiencies, suggested amendment to and why it's necessary to fix the situation.

Common Soil Deficiencies & Suggested Amendments

Nitrogen (N)	Ammonium nitrate, Urea, Compost	Increases leafy growth and overall plant vigor
Phosphorus (P)	Bone meal, Rock phosphate, Superphosphate	Essential for root development and flowering

Potassium (K)	Potassium sulfate, Potassium chloride (muriate of potash)	Important for flowering, fruiting, and overall health
Calcium (Ca)	Gypsum, Lime, Dolomitic lime	Crucial for cell wall structure and enzyme activity
Magnesium (Mg)	Epsom salts (magnesium sulfate), Dolomitic lime	Key for photosynthesis and enzyme systems
Sulfur (S)	Gypsum, Elemental sulfur, Ammonium sulfate	Necessary for protein production and enzyme activities
Iron (Fe)	Iron sulfate, Chelated iron	Important for chlorophyll synthesis and enzyme function
Zinc (Zn)	Zinc sulfate, Chelated zinc	Crucial for growth hormone production and enzyme systems

Whether your soil is too sandy or too clay-like, the best fix is to add compost, manure, and leaf mold. Using straw, bark, wood chips or grass clippings as organic mulch will help retain soil moisture and suppress weeds. In fact, just always add organic matter. You can't go wrong.

Fertilizers - The N-P-K Ratio

The most prominent feature on a fertilizer bag is the N-P-K ratio, which stands for Nitrogen (N), Phosphorus (P), and Potassium (K). These numbers are percentages by weight of each nutrient.

- **Nitrogen (N)** is essential for leafy growth and green color.
- **Phosphorus (P)** helps with root development, flowering, and fruiting.
- **Potassium (K)** contributes to overall plant health and resistance to disease.

For example, a fertilizer with a label saying "10-20-10" contains 10% nitrogen, 20% phosphorus, and 10% potassium. The rest of the product is usually filler material that helps distribute the nutrients or may contain other minor or trace nutrients.

Typically, a balanced fertilizer is commonly recommended for general vegetable garden use such as a **10-10-10 or 20-20-20** ratio.

Additional Nutrients

Some fertilizers also contain other essential nutrients like calcium (Ca), magnesium (Mg), and sulfur (S), along with trace elements like iron (Fe), zinc (Zn), manganese (Mn), and copper (Cu). These will be listed separately, often with their percentage by weight or in parts per million (ppm).

Application Instructions

The label will include detailed instructions on how to apply the fertilizer, including:

- **Application rates:** Specifies how much of the product to use per unit area (e.g., pounds per 1000 square feet).
- **Timing:** Indicates the best time of year or stage of plant growth for application.
- **Method:** Describes how to apply the fertilizer (e.g., broadcasting, side-dressing, or diluting in water for a liquid feed).

Crop Rotation – The Benefits

Crop rotation is an age-old practice that's still the "Must Do" for all gardens. It's all about moving your veggies around in a planned sequence each season. This isn't just to keep them guessing – there are proven benefits.

Improved Soil Health and Fertility

Different crops have varying nutrient requirements and rooting depths. By rotating crops, the nutrient usage is balanced, preventing the depletion of specific soil nutrients. For example, legumes (like beans and peas) can fix atmospheric nitrogen, enriching the soil with this crucial nutrient for plant growth. Following legumes with nitrogen-loving crops (such as corn or leafy greens) can take advantage of this natural soil enrichment. Additionally, the diversity of root systems improves soil structure, enhances water infiltration, and reduces erosion.

Pest and Disease Management

Many pests and diseases are host-specific, meaning they prefer specific crops or plant families. By rotating crops, you break the life cycles of these pests and diseases, reducing their buildup in the soil and lowering the incidence of outbreaks. This can lead to a decrease in the need for chemical pesticides, contributing to a healthier environment and potentially reducing farming costs. For instance, rotating away from a crop that a particular pest favors, can starve that pest population, leading to a natural decline in its numbers.

Increased Crop Yield

The combination of improved soil health, reduced pest and disease pressure, and the optimal use of soil nutrients leads to a healthier growing environment for crops, which can result in increased yields. A common rotation sequence follows a four-year plan: leafy greens, fruits (like tomatoes and peppers), roots, and then legumes to fix nitrogen back into the soil.

To make rotation work, you need to be organized. Use your logbook or a garden journal detailing what was planted where and when. This record-keeping is your roadmap for future planting, ensuring that no area of your garden is overworked.

Companion Planting

Think of companion planting as setting up a buddy system for your plants. Placing certain plants side-by-side is like setting up a neighborhood watch for your garden. This method involves strategic positioning of flora that emit natural substances in their roots or foliage to repel pests, attract beneficial insects, or even improve the growth and flavor of their garden neighbors.

Certain plant pairings are like best friends—they bring out the best in each other. Tomatoes love being near basil, and carrots are happy next to onions. These companions can help deter pests, improve pollination, and even enhance the flavor of their garden-mates. But be wary of incompatible pairings—some plants just don't get along. For example, keep your dill far away from your carrots. Separate tomatoes and potatoes, as well as onions and beans. These unfriendly neighbors can stunt each other's growth or attract the wrong kind of bugs.

Friendly Companions	Unfriendly Vegetables
Tomatoes & Basil	Tomatoes & Potatoes
Carrots & Onions	Carrots & Parsnips & Dill
Lettuce & Radishes	Lettuce & Celery
Cucumbers & Beans	Cucumbers & Potatoes
Peppers & Basil	Peppers & Fennel

Corn & Beans & Squash	Corn & Tomatoes
Spinach & Strawberries	Spinach & Potatoes
Beets & Garlic	Beets & Pole Beans

Plants that Repel Insects

Speaking of insects, the following is a list of plants that naturally repel insects. This can be an effective way to protect your vegetable garden from pests without resorting to chemical pesticides. Here's a list of plants known for their bug-deterring properties:

1. **Marigolds:** The scent of marigolds is believed to repel aphids, mosquitoes, and exude a substance that deters nematodes. Planting marigolds around the perimeter of your garden or between vegetable rows can help protect your crops.

2. **Basil:** Known to repel flies and mosquitoes, basil can be a great companion for tomatoes, enhancing their growth and flavor while keeping pests away.

3. **Lavender:** Lavender's strong scent deters moths, fleas, flies, and mosquitoes. Planting lavender around your garden can help create a pest-resistant barrier.

4. **Chrysanthemums:** These flowers contain a compound called pyrethrin, used in many insect repellents and insecticides. They're effective against beetles, ants, and roaches.

5. **Mint:** While mint can repel several insect pests, including mosquitoes, it's best planted in pots around the garden to prevent it from spreading aggressively.

6. **Rosemary:** This herb repels a variety of insects harmful to vegetable plants, including cabbage moths and carrot flies. It's particularly beneficial for beans, cabbage, and carrots.

7. **Lemongrass:** Containing citronella, a natural mosquito repellent, lemongrass can be planted in pots and placed strategically around the garden because of its tendency to be invasive.

8. **Garlic:** Planting garlic around your garden can help repel pests like aphids, Japanese beetles, and carrot root flies. It's particularly beneficial for roses and raspberries.

9. **Catnip:** Known to be more effective than DEET in repelling mosquitoes, catnip can also deter a variety of other insects. However, it may attract cats to your garden.

10. **Petunias:** Often referred to as "nature's pesticide," petunias repel aphids, tomato hornworms, asparagus beetles, leafhoppers, and squash bugs.

Seasonal Planting Schedule

Timing is everything in your garden. A seasonal planting schedule is your planting and harvesting playbook, tailored to your local climate. It dictates when to sow seeds indoors to get a jump on the season, when to transplant seedlings outside, and when to direct sow in the ground.

Use your region's last frost date in spring and first frost date in fall as benchmarks. These dates bracket your growing season and are critical for planning. Some crops, like peas and spinach, love the cool start of spring, while others, such as corn and tomatoes, need the warm soil of late spring or early summer.

Garden Layout Log

- **Sunny Spots:** Marked areas for sun-loving crops.
- **Shaded Areas:** Designated for shade-tolerant plants.
- **Water Source:** Location relative to garden.

Crafting a garden on your homestead is a deliberate process—a blend of art, science, and a touch of intuition. It's about understanding the unique characteristics of your land and working with them to create a space where plants can thrive. With careful planning and a dash of creativity, your garden will become a source of pride and sustenance, a verdant corner of your homestead that nourishes both body and soul.

Climate Specific Farming Techniques

Your homestead's locale dictates the rhythms of your daily life, and nowhere is this more apparent than in the garden. Each climate niche presents its unique set of challenges, but with a keen eye and a bit of innovation, you can tailor your farming techniques to turn potential obstacles into advantageous strategies.

Dry Farming in Arid Regions

In regions where rain is a rare guest, the earth's natural moisture becomes a precious commodity. Dry farming is an approach that maximizes this resource, focusing on water retention in the soil and selecting crops that thrive with minimal hydration. Here, the secret lies in timing and soil preparation. Plant your seeds right after the rainy season to capitalize on the moisture that's soaked into the ground. Then, cultivate your soil to create a fine dust mulch layer—this acts as a barrier, reducing evaporation. Deep, infrequent watering encourages plants to develop extensive root systems, delving deep for water and nutrients. Hardy varieties of tomatoes, squash, and melons often excel in these conditions, having adapted to make the most of less.

Raised Beds in Wet Climates

When the rains are frequent visitors, the challenge becomes not retaining moisture but ensuring adequate drainage. Raised beds rise to the occasion, elevating your plants above the soggy embrace of the earth. Construct these beds with non-toxic materials such as untreated hardwood, composite materials – a mix of wood fiber and plastic, galvanized steel or concrete blocks. Railroad ties contain creosote, which is toxic and should be avoided.

Fill your raised garden beds with a blend of soil and compost. The elevation prevents water from pooling around the roots, warding off rot and fungal diseases that can spell disaster for your crops. Raised beds also warm up faster in the spring, giving you a head start on the growing season. With the added benefit of being easier on the back during planting and weeding, they present a practical solution for those dealing with persistent dampness.

Greenhouses in Cold Climates

When winter's chill lingers and frost threatens to nip your tender seedlings, greenhouses offer a sanctuary of warmth. Acting as sun catchers, they trap heat during the day and maintain a stable environment that shields plants from the bitter cold. The choice of glazing—be it glass or polycarbonate—plays a crucial role in insulation. Inside, you can cultivate a variety of plants that would otherwise shiver and falter in the open air. Tomatoes, cucumbers, and peppers can thrive year-round with the right management. Ventilation is key to preventing overheating and humidity buildup; automatic vent openers can regulate temperature without daily fuss.

Shade Cloth in Hot Climates

Conversely, in areas where the sun beats down with relentless intensity, shade cloth stands as a defender against the scorch. Draped over your plants, these woven screens filter the sunlight, reducing heat stress and preventing scorching. They come in various densities, allowing you to customize the level of protection based on the needs of your crops. Lettuce, spinach, and other greens are particularly grateful for the reprieve from the heat. Shade cloth can also reduce water loss from evaporation, making your irrigation efforts more effective. Its use is not limited to the hottest months; retractable systems can offer versatility, providing shade as needed throughout the growing season.

Each of these techniques embraces the local climate, turning what might seem like limitations into strengths. They're not just strategies but also expressions of respect for the land and its conditions. By adapting your approach to the unique rhythms of your homestead's locale, you create a garden that's in harmony with the environment, yielding a bounty that reflects both your dedication and the natural world's resilience.

Extending the Growing Season

Every homesteader knows the bittersweet feeling as the warmth of summer gives way to the crisp air of autumn. But what if you could capture a few more weeks of growth, or even make your garden yield produce throughout the year? Extending the growing season is not mere wishful thinking—it's a reality achieved through structures and techniques designed to shield your plants from the elements and provide them a microclimate where they can continue to thrive.

Cold Frames

Cold frames are like mini greenhouses nestled directly on your garden beds. They consist of a transparent lid, often angled towards the sun, set atop a sturdy, insulated frame. Think of them as cozy winter jackets for your plants, trapping solar heat and maintaining a snug environment even as the temperature outside dips. Construct these frames from durable materials like wood or bricks, and use old windows or clear polycarbonate sheets for the lid.

Plant cold-hardy veggies like kale, chard, or spinach inside these frames, and they'll keep producing well into the colder months. The key is to regulate the temperature—prop open the lid during the day to prevent overheating and close it tight at night to retain warmth. It's a simple, energy-free solution that can make a world of difference in extending your harvest time.

Hoop Houses

Hoop houses offer you a step up in size and protection. These tunnel-like structures, created by bending metal pipes or PVC into arches and covering them with plastic sheeting, stand guard over your crops. Inside, the air warms up during the day, and the soil stays soft, allowing for a prolonged growing period.

You can walk right in, tend to your plants, or even set up raised beds within this protective cocoon. Ventilation is facilitated by rolling up the sides or employing end-wall windows. When winter looms, double up the plastic or add a layer of row covers inside for extra insulation, turning your hoop house into a stronghold against the frost.

Greenhouses

Consider greenhouses the crown jewels of season extension. These structures are more permanent and can be outfitted with heating systems, allowing you to defy winter's grip entirely. With a greenhouse, you're not just extending the season; you're creating a whole new climate zone on your homestead.

Different styles cater to diverse needs and budgets, from simple plastic-covered frames to elaborate glasshouses with automated controls. Inside, you can start seedlings early, grow warmth-loving plants year-round, and experiment with varieties your local climate would never typically allow. Remember, managing a greenhouse is a balancing act—you'll need to monitor humidity, provide adequate water, and ensure proper ventilation to prevent diseases.

Indoor Gardening

When the outdoors becomes inhospitable, bring the garden inside. Indoor gardening is not just for the urban dweller with window boxes of herbs. Even on a homestead, dedicating space indoors for growing can lead to impressive yields. LED grow lights mimic the spectrum of the sun, and with these, an indoor garden need not even be near a window.

Indoor options range from hydroponic systems, where plants grow in nutrient-rich water, to traditional pots filled with soil. Vertical towers or shelves maximize space, allowing for a lush indoor landscape of herbs, greens, and even some fruiting plants like peppers or dwarf tomatoes. The beauty of indoor gardening is the control it provides—temperature, light, and water are all at your discretion, meaning you can harvest fresh produce even as snow blankets the ground outside.

Extending the growing season is a testament to human ingenuity and the drive for self-sufficiency. It's about adapting to the challenges of the climate and finding innovative ways to maintain and increase productivity. With each of these methods, you create pockets of warmth and life, ensuring that the gifts of the garden can be enjoyed for as long as possible, and sometimes, even against the odds, throughout the entire year.

Pest Control and Organic Farming Methods

In the ebb and flow of homestead life, there's a natural rhythm to pest control and the nurturing of crops that doesn't rely on synthetic chemicals. As mentioned earlier while discussing crop rotation, it's about fostering an environment where your plants can grow robust and resilient, capable of standing firm against the nibbles and gnaws of the local fauna. Here, we focus on methods that align with the cycles of nature, fortifying your garden with defenses that are as organic as the soil beneath your boots.

Natural Pesticides

When pests do make their unwelcome appearance, reach for solutions that Mother Nature herself might concoct. Neem oil, extracted from the seeds of the neem tree, is a marvel of the organic arsenal, dealing a blow to insects at various life stages. A dusting of diatomaceous earth, comprised of fossilized remains of tiny aquatic organisms, can deter crawling pests with its abrasive texture. Sprays made from fermented garlic or hot pepper serve as spicy deterrents that many pests find unpalatable. These natural concoctions offer targeted action without lingering in the ecosystem.

Beneficial Insects

Recruiting an army of beneficial insects to your garden is like enlisting nature's own pest patrol.

Ladybugs (Lady Beetles) are voracious predators of aphids and other soft-bodied pests. If there is a steady food source, ladybugs can stay in the garden for several weeks, especially if they are in their larval stage, which is also predatory. However, adult ladybugs may disperse in search of new feeding grounds or suitable overwintering sites once the prey becomes scarce or environmental conditions change.

Green lacewings, whose larvae are known as "aphid lions" for their appetite for aphids, can remain in the garden for their entire larval stage (2-3 weeks) if food is abundant. After maturing into adults, they might stay if there is enough food and suitable conditions for laying eggs.

Predatory mites are used to control spider mites and other pest mites. They will stay in the area as long as there is a food source. Without food or if conditions become unfavorable (e.g., too hot, too dry), they may die off or leave the area.

Parasitoid Wasps lay their eggs in or on pests like caterpillars, aphids, and beetle larvae. The lifespan and residency of parasitoid wasps in your garden depend on the presence of host pests for their offspring. If hosts are plentiful, they can stay and reproduce over multiple generations within a season.

General Tips to Retain Beneficial Insects:

Provide a habitat: Planting a variety of flowers, especially those with umbel-shaped blooms like dill, parsley, and fennel, can provide nectar and pollen for adult beneficial insects, encouraging them to stay longer.

Ensure a continuous food supply: A diverse garden with a mix of plants can support a range of pests, which in turn can feed beneficial insects throughout the growing season.

Avoid pesticides: Even organic pesticides can harm beneficial insects. Using pesticides may reduce the food available to beneficial insects, causing them to leave or die off.

Water sources: Providing shallow water sources can help beneficial insects stay hydrated, especially during hot, dry periods.

Ultimately, the key to keeping beneficial insects in your garden longer is to create an environment that meets their needs for food, water, and shelter.

Physical Barriers

Sometimes the best offense is a good defense, and in the garden, this can mean erecting physical barriers. Floating row covers, made of lightweight fabric, let sunlight and water in while keeping pests out. For burrowing creatures, a fence dug into the soil can be a formidable underground wall. And for your fruit trees, a simple band of sticky material around the trunk can trap crawling insects before they reach the canopy.

As the day wanes and a quiet peace settles over your garden, you can take solace in the knowledge that your organic methods are working in concert with nature to create a healthy, vibrant ecosystem. These techniques, woven into the fabric of your daily routines, build a garden that's not only productive but also a sanctuary for the beneficial creatures that help maintain balance. Your efforts here are part of a larger commitment to stewardship, to a way of life that respects and protects the intricate web of life that thrives in your care.

In the days to come, as you watch the fruits of your labor take shape in the ripening tomatoes and the sprouting beans, remember that each choice you make echoes through the soil, the plants, and the pollinators that visit your blossoms. Your garden is a microcosm of the world outside its borders, a place where the harmonious interplay of all living things is not just observed but actively encouraged.

With the garden established and defended, our gaze shifts next to the harvest and beyond—to the preservation of its bounty, ensuring the wealth of the seasons extends its reach into the quiet of winter and the promise of the meals to come.

References:

Almanac.com Garden Plans for Homesteads and Small Farms - https://www.almanac.com/garden-plans-homesteads-and-small-farms

The World Bank - Climate-Smart Agriculture (CSA) is an integrated approach to managing landscapes that addresses the interlinked challenges of food security and climate change. - https://www.worldbank.org/en/topic/climate-smart-agriculture

Season Extension through Protected Cultivation & 10 Season-Extension Suggestions. - https://www.johnnyseeds.com/growers-library/methods-tools-supplies/winter-growing-season-extension/10-ways-extend-your-season.html

Organic Pest Control Methods - https://extension.sdstate.edu/organic-pest-control-methods

Benefits of Companion Planting - https://homesteadandchill.com/benefits-companion-planting-chart/

Relevant Resources:

There are literally hundreds of books on gardening – these are some of my favorite websites

Farmers Almanac: https://www.almanac.com/

GardenBeast (Ebooks) - 7 Free Gardening Ebooks

National Gardening Association - https://garden.org/

Garden Betty - https://www.gardenbetty.com Advice on chickens also.

A Way to Garden - https://awaytogarden.com

Tiny Farm Blog - https://tinyfarmblog.com/

Year-Round Food Production

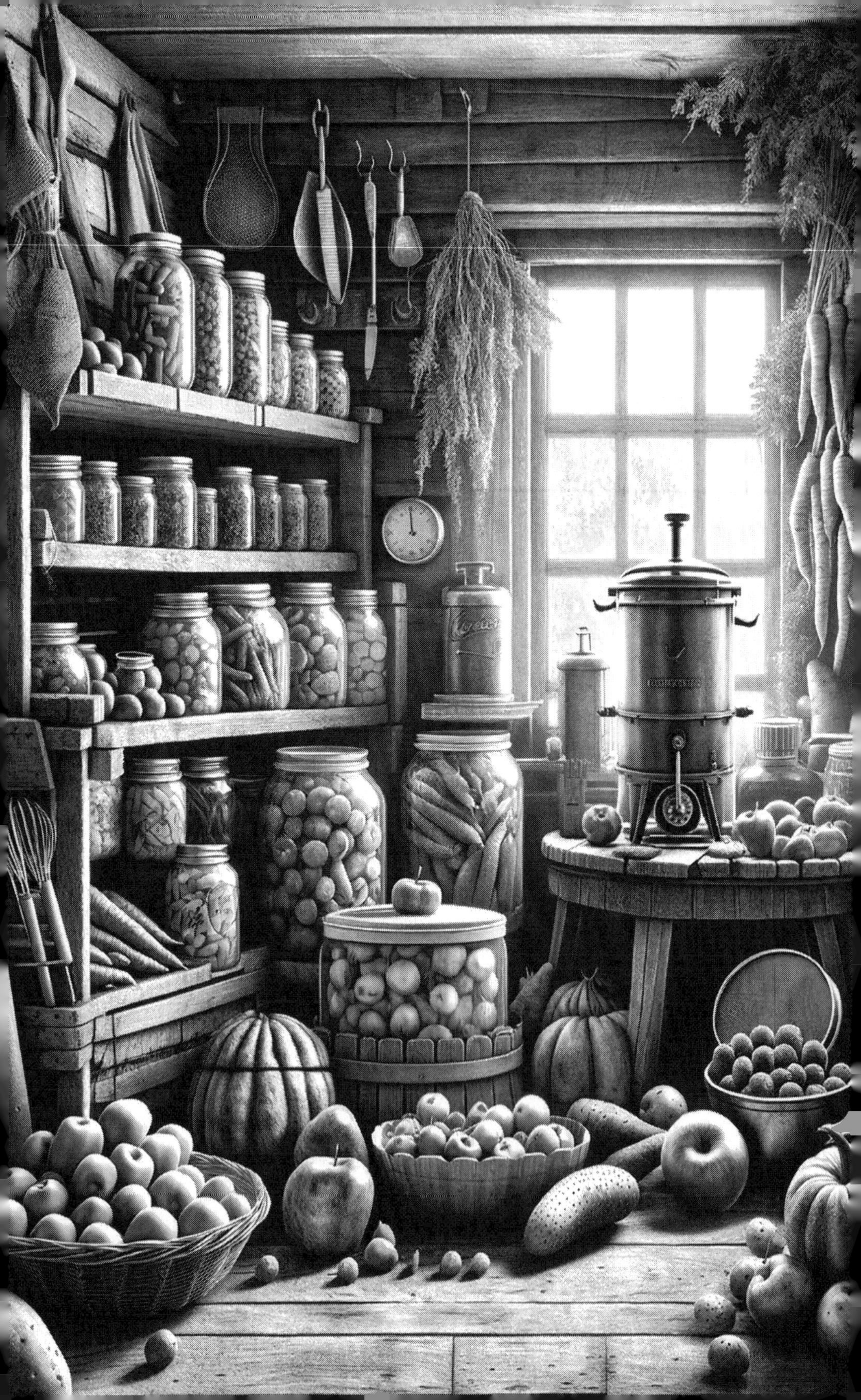

Chapter 8
Preserving the Harvest: Canning and Storing Your Produce

The aroma of simmering tomatoes, the crisp snap of a fresh green bean, the earthy sweetness of just-dug carrots—these are the fleeting perfumes of the harvest. Yet, through the alchemy of canning, you need not say farewell to these sensory delights as the seasons turn. Canning is the homesteader's time capsule, a way to capture the essence of summer's bounty and savor it in the depths of winter's chill. It's a bridge between the abundance of now and the scarcity of later, a method steeped in tradition but just as relevant today in our quest for a sustainable, self-sufficient lifestyle.

Treasure these moments, when your kitchen becomes a hub of transformation, where the fruits of your labor are sealed within glass walls, ready to be awakened at your will. Embrace the rhythm of this ancient dance, from the preparation of produce to the sealing of lids and let the comforting clatter of jars and the hiss of escaping steam be the soundtrack to your preservation endeavors.

Home Canning Basics

Canning is not just a means to an end—it's an invitation to engage with your food on a deeper level. It's a commitment to quality and a nod to the old ways, ensuring that each jar you seal is a testament to your dedication.

Water Bath Canning is perfect for high-acid foods like fruits, jams, and pickles. The acidity, combined with heat, is enough to ward off spoilage and keep your food safe. Submerge your filled jars in a pot of boiling water, ensuring they're completely covered. The rolling boil drives out air and creates a vacuum seal as the jars cool.

Pressure Canning is used for low-acid foods like vegetables and meats, pressure canning is your go-to method. It involves a specialized pressure canner that reaches higher temperatures than boiling water alone, annihilating any botulism spores that might be lurking. It's a bit like a spa-day for your jars, except instead of relaxation, they're getting a thorough, bacteria-killing heat treatment.

Jar Selection and Preparation

- **Choosing Jars:** Always opt for jars specifically designed for canning—no repurposing old mayonnaise jars here. Typical brand names include Mason or Ball jars. They come in various sizes, from pint to quart, and it's essential to select the size that matches your recipe's recommendations.

- **Preparation:** Begin by inspecting your jars for nicks or cracks; even a small imperfection can compromise the seal. Wash them in hot, soapy water or run them through the dishwasher. For hot packing, keep jars warm to prevent thermal shock when you add your piping hot product.

Safety Guidelines

- **Sterilization:** Before filling, sterilize your jars if the processing time will be less than 10 minutes. You can do this by boiling them or using the sterilize cycle on your dishwasher.

- **Headspace:** That little bit of space between the food and the jar's rim is critical. Too little, and the contents might bubble over during processing; too much, and the jar may not seal properly.

- **Bubble Removal:** After filling, run a nonmetallic spatula around the inside edge of the jar to release trapped air bubbles—a crucial step to ensure proper vacuum sealing.

- **Wiping Rims:** Any residue on the jar rim can prevent a proper seal. Wipe the rims with a clean, damp cloth before placing the lid.
- **Finger-Tight:** When you screw on the band, aim for "finger-tight." Over-tightening can prevent air from escaping, leading to a faulty seal.
- **Steps:**
    1. Select and prepare your jars.
    2. Fill jars with product, leaving appropriate headspace.
    3. Remove air bubbles and wipe rims.
    4. Apply lids and screw bands until finger-tight.
    5. Process jars using water bath or pressure canning method.
    6. Cool jars and check seals.

Canning Readiness Checklist

- Jars, lids, and bands inspected and cleaned
- Canning tools (jar lifter, funnel, spatula) at the ready
- Recipe ingredients prepped and measured
- Workspace organized and clean
- Safety guidelines reviewed

The Importance of Acidity in Canning

Understanding the role of acidity in canning is crucial—it's the shield that guards against spoilage. High-acid foods naturally create an inhospitable environment for bacteria, while low-acid foods rely on the intense heat of pressure canning to ensure safety. Always use tested recipes and never alter the proportions of acidic to non-acidic ingredients.

Canning is a dance of precision and patience, a ritual that binds us to the cycles of nature and the bounty of the earth. It is a celebration of the harvest and a pledge to honor the gifts of the land. Each jar you seal is a story—a story of growth, of care, and of the quiet satisfaction that comes with self-sufficiency. So, as you line your pantry shelves with gleaming jars of preserved goodness, take pride in this connection to the past and the security it brings to your future.

Dehydrating Fruits and Vegetables

The preservation of produce through dehydration is an age-old practice, and its relevance endures in the modern homestead. This method of food preservation removes moisture from fruits and vegetables, inhibiting the growth of bacteria and mold. The result is a lightweight, nutrient-dense, and shelf-stable provision that is as versatile as it is delicious. Engage in the process of drying your harvest and you'll soon discover the ease with which you can stock your pantry with snacks, ingredients for cooking, and emergency food supplies.

Choosing a Dehydrator

Selecting the right dehydrator can feel like finding the perfect tool for a craftsman. It must meet the demands of your harvest and suit the rhythms of your household. Dehydrators come in many forms, from stackable electric models with trays that allow warm air to circulate vertically, to larger box-and-shelf units where air moves horizontally, providing an even and consistent dry environment. Consider the following when making your choice:

Capacity: Match the dehydrator's size to your typical batch of produce. Larger units can handle bountiful harvests, while compact models suffice for smaller batches.

Airflow and Heat Distribution: Uniform drying is key; models with a fan located in the back tend to distribute heat more evenly than those with fans at the bottom or top.

Thermostat and Timer: Adjustable temperature control allows for precision in drying different types of produce, while a timer ensures the process can run unattended without the risk of over-drying.

Preparing Produce for Dehydration

With your dehydrator selected, turn your attention to the fruits and vegetables destined for drying. Each item requires a unique approach to preparation:

- **Washing:** Begin by thoroughly cleaning your produce to remove any dirt or pesticides. Organic or not, cleanliness is paramount.
- **Slicing:** Uniformity in slice thickness leads to even drying. Use a mandoline or sharp knife for consistency.

- **Blanching:** Some vegetables benefit from a quick blanching before drying. This step can halt enzyme activity that may cause unfavorable changes in flavor and color.
- **Pre-Treating:** Certain fruits like apples and bananas may darken during drying. A dip in lemon juice or ascorbic acid solution can preserve their natural hues.

Storing Dehydrated Foods

After dehydration, turn to the task of storage, which ensures the longevity and quality of your dried goods. Airtight containers are essential, safeguarding the food from moisture and pests. Use glass jars, vacuum-sealed bags, or plastic containers with tight-fitting lids. Keep these containers in a cool, dark place to maintain the integrity of the dried produce. Exposure to heat or light can diminish nutritional value and lead to spoilage. For added protection, consider using oxygen absorbers, which remove air from the storage container, further extending the shelf life of the dehydrated items.

Rehydrating Foods

The beauty of dehydrated foods lies not only in their storage longevity but also in their ability to be rejuvenated. Rehydrating dried fruits and vegetables is straightforward:

- **Soaking:** Submerge the dried produce in water, juice, or broth, giving it time to absorb the liquid and plump up. The soaking time will vary depending on the size and type of produce.
- **Cooking:** You can also add dried produce directly to soups, stews, or other cooked dishes. They will rehydrate as they simmer, absorbing flavors from the dish and contributing their own.
- **Temperature:** Warm or hot liquids will speed up the rehydration process, while cold liquids may be used when a slower absorption is desired or to maintain a firmer texture.

Dried fruits and vegetables retain much of their nutritional value and can be a convenient option for snacking, cooking, or as part of your emergency food stash. Their versatility and ease of use make dehydrating an attractive option for homesteaders looking to preserve their harvest in a sustainable and practical manner. Whether enjoyed as a chewy snack during a hike, tossed into a winter stew, or rehydrated into a summer fruit salad, the dehydrated produce from your homestead garden can be a source of pride and sustenance throughout the year.

Root Cellaring Techniques

Venturing beneath the frost line, where the earth remains a stable temperature year-round, we uncover the age-old practice of root cellaring. This method, a natural form of refrigeration has been trusted by generations to preserve the integrity of the harvest without the need for electricity. Root cellars are subterranean sanctuaries for vegetables, offering an environment conducive to prolonging freshness and vitality.

Ideal Location for a Root Cellar

In selecting the perfect spot for a root cellar, one must consider accessibility and environmental conditions. A north-facing slope is often the prime choice, taking advantage of natural insulation provided by the earth. Proximity to your home is practical for ease of access during inclement weather. The cellar should be situated at a depth where the soil temperature remains constant, avoiding areas where the water table is high to prevent flooding.

Incorporating existing structures can be beneficial; the north side of a barn or the unused space beneath a porch can be transformed into an effective storage area. For those building a cellar from scratch, careful planning ensures that the location meets the criteria for darkness, coolness, and moisture which are intrinsic to a successful root cellar.

Proper Ventilation

Maintaining air quality inside a root cellar is critical to prevent the buildup of ethylene gas and moisture, which can accelerate spoilage. Strategic ventilation provides a pathway for these gases to escape. This can be achieved by installing vents that draw in cooler air from outside at one end of the cellar and expel warmer air through a higher vent on the opposite end, creating a natural convection current.

The size and number of vents will depend on the cellar's volume; a general rule of thumb is to have at least one square foot of vent per 100 square feet of floor space. Adjustable covers for the vents allow you to regulate airflow in response to external temperatures, ensuring the optimal climate is maintained within the cellar.

Storage Containers

The choice of containers for storing your harvest is more than a matter of convenience; it's a factor that can impact the longevity of your produce. Wooden crates and bushel baskets are preferred for their breathability, allowing air to circulate around the produce. Bins constructed of wire mesh or slatted wood also serve this purpose well.

When arranging these containers, allow for space between them to enable airflow and prevent the accumulation of moisture. Shelves or stacking bins can help organize the space, keeping different types of produce separated to reduce the risk of cross-contamination from any spoiled items.

Temperature and Humidity Control

Controlling the temperature and humidity in a root cellar is similar to setting the stage for a long performance – it requires constant attention to detail. The ideal temperature range lies between 32°F and 40°F, cool enough to slow decay but above freezing. Humidity levels should hover around 85% to 95%, keeping produce from drying out but not so damp as to encourage mold growth.

In managing these conditions, the earth itself is an ally. Its insulating properties can help buffer the cellar from temperature swings. Inside, a thick layer of straw or sawdust on the floor can help maintain humidity, while a simple thermometer and hygrometer will monitor the environment. During warmer months, barrels of water can absorb excess heat, and during cooler periods, insulating blankets or additional layers of soil on the cellar's roof can provide extra warmth.

The root cellar, then, is not just a storage space – it's a living environment that requires a harmonious balance of elements. It's a place where the robust flavors of autumn can be cradled through the winter, ready to emerge as a reminder of the past season's labor. Here, in the quiet darkness beneath the frost, the fruits of your work are preserved, a connection to the land that endures even as the world above sleeps under a blanket of snow.

Safe Food Storage Practices

Securing the longevity of your stored food necessitates a blend of attentiveness and know-how. It begins with the meticulous sealing of canning lids, ensuring each jar is airtight. The process requires precision; lids must be centered and tightened just so, creating an environment free from external contaminants. A well-sealed lid will have a concave shape, indicating a successful seal, allowing for the preservation of the contents within.

Once sealed, the environment in which these jars are kept plays a pivotal role. Fluctuations in temperature and humidity can compromise the integrity of your preserves, leading to potential spoilage. A cool, dry area is the sanctuary for these vessels, away from the light which could degrade the quality of the food over time. Basements, cellars, or dedicated pantry rooms are often ideal, maintaining a consistent atmosphere that supports extended storage.

The duty of care extends to regular inspection of stored foods. Vigilance is key; a routine survey of your jars for signs of spoilage such as cloudiness, leakage, or rust ensures any compromised goods are removed, protecting the remainder. This process not only guarantees the safety of the preserved bounty but also fosters a relationship between the homesteader and their provisions, each jar a chapter in the story of the season's yield.

Rotation of stored foods is another pillar of effective preservation. By organizing your stores so that older items are in front and newer ones in the back, you ensure a cycle of usage that prevents any from lingering past their prime. This method, known as 'first-in, first-out,' is a discipline that pays dividends in minimizing waste and maximizing the enjoyment of each harvest.

Finally, the matter of pest prevention is not to be overlooked. Creatures great and small are drawn to the fruits of your labor, making it imperative to safeguard your stores. Secure containers, free from cracks or gaps, are the first line of defense. Regular cleaning of storage areas dissuades invaders, while natural deterrents such as bay leaves or cedar blocks can be strategically placed to ward off would-be intruders.

Through the adoption of these practices, the treasures of your harvest are well-guarded, ready to be awakened to enrich meals and nourish through the leaner times. The diligence in these tasks reflects the broader ethos of the homestead—a commitment to a life woven with the threads of sustainability, resilience, and respect for the bounty the earth provides.

As the chapter on preservation closes, we carry with us the knowledge that the fruits of our labor can be extended beyond their natural season. We hold the assurance that our efforts today lay the foundation for the nourishment of tomorrow. Ahead lies the promise of security, the joy of sharing, and the satisfaction of a pantry well-stocked with the colors and flavors of the harvest, encapsulating the very essence of homesteading.

References:

USDA Complete Guide to Home Canning, 2015 revision - https://nchfp.uga.edu/publications/publications_usda.html

We Tested 12 Food Dehydrators—Here Are Our Favorite Models - https://www.seriouseats.com/best-food-dehydrators-5216308

The Ultimate Guide to Root Cellars: How to Build and Maintain Your Own - https://modernwarriorproject.com/root-cellars/

Long Term Food Storage: Best Containers and Treatment Methods - https://theprovidentprepper.org/long-term-food-storage-best-containers-and-treatment-methods/

Relevant Resources:

Cookbooks about Canning, Preserving Foods, Curing Meats, Making Cheese are readily available in most bookstores and Amazon.

Suggested Cookbooks include:

Better Homes and Gardens: Complete Canning Guide

The Farmer's Kitchen Handbook: More Than 200 Recipes for Making Cheese, Curing Meat, Preserving, Fermenting, and More

Home Cheese Making, 4th Edition: From Fresh and Soft to Firm, Blue, Goat's Milk, and More; Recipes for 100 Favorite Cheeses

The Complete Guide to Smoking and Salt Curing: How to Preserve Meat, Fish, and Game

Living Off-Grid: Homesteading 101

Chapter 9
Raising and Harvesting Chickens for the Homestead

Introduction

Primary reasons for raising chickens on a homestead is to provide fresh eggs and meat. Unlike store-bought alternatives, eggs from backyard chickens are more nutritious, boasting brighter yolks and higher levels of vitamins and omega-3 fatty acids. The meat from home-raised chickens is also of superior quality, with the added advantage of knowing exactly what the birds have been fed and how they have been treated throughout their lives.

So, do you need a rooster? No. No rooster, no problem. A hen does not need a rooster to ovulate. You only need a rooster in order to mate with a hen to produce fertile eggs.

Which Breed of Chicken is Best for Your Homestead?

Choosing the Right Breed: Choosing the right breed of chicken for your homestead involves considering several factors, including the climate of your area, the primary purpose of raising chickens (eggs, meat, or both), and the temperament suited to your living situation.

Climate Adaptability: Cold climates look for breeds with smaller combs and wattles to reduce frostbite risk, and those with thick feathering for warmth. Examples include the Plymouth Rock, Wyandotte, and Orpington. Whereas for hotter climates chickens with larger combs and wattles for better heat dissipation and lighter feathering. Leghorns and Rhode Island Reds are good choices for warmer areas.

Egg Production: If your main goal is a high yield of eggs, consider White Leghorns for white eggs and Rhode Island Reds and Australorps known for their brown eggs. These breeds can lay up to 250-300 eggs per year. It's important to note that egg production peaks in the first two years of a hen's life and gradually decreases afterward.

Egg Color Variety: For a colorful egg basket, consider Araucanas, Ameraucanas, or Cream Legbars, which lay blue and green eggs. Average annual egg production ranges between 150 -180 eggs per year.

Meat Yield: For homesteaders raising chickens primarily for meat, breeds with rapid growth rates and substantial body size are preferred. Cornish Crosses are the most common meat breed, known for their fast growth and substantial meat yield. The heritage breeds like the Jersey Giant and the Orpington grow slower than broilers but are prized for their flavor and texture.

Temperament: The breed's temperament is crucial, especially if the chickens will be integrated into a family setting with children or other animals. Some docile breeds include Brahmas and Buff Orpingtons and are excellent pets. The Leghorns and Anconas are more independent and less interested in human interaction, which might be preferable for some setups.

Dual-Purpose Breeds: If you're looking for versatility, several breeds offer both respectable egg production and meat yield. You should look at the Plymouth Rocks, Sussex, and Wyandotte's which provide a balanced mix of egg-laying capabilities and meat.

When selecting a breed, consider visiting local farms or poultry shows to observe the chickens firsthand and speak with experienced breeders. They can offer insights into how different breeds might fit into your homestead's environment and your lifestyle.

Chickens' Quirky Behavior:

Chickens exhibit a range of quirky behaviors that can be both amusing and perplexing. Understanding these behaviors can enhance the experience of raising chickens and provide insight into their social structure and individual personalities. Here are some notable quirky behaviors:

Dust Bathing: Chickens love to bathe in dust. They will find a dry, dusty spot and create a shallow pit, then roll, flap, and shake in it. This behavior helps them to maintain their feather health and rid themselves of parasites.

Coming Home to Roost: Chickens will always come home at night once they identify their coop as home. They have a favorite spot on the roost, and roosting buddy. Higher roosts are considered more safe from predators.

Sunbathing: Chickens often stretch out one wing and leg to soak up the sun, looking almost as if they are sunbathing. This behavior not only helps them regulate their body temperature but also aids in vitamin D synthesis.

The Egg Song: After laying an egg, a hen often announces her accomplishment with a series of loud and distinctive clucks known as the "egg song." It's a peculiar behavior that can rally the whole flock into a chorus.

Pecking Order: Chickens have a complex social hierarchy known as the "pecking order." This order determines access to food, nesting sites, and roosting spots. Watching chickens establish and navigate this hierarchy can be quite entertaining.

Following the Leader: Chickens tend to follow their keeper or a dominant chicken around, often in a line. This behavior showcases their social nature and tendency to form strong flock dynamics.

Tidbitting: Roosters perform a dance known as "tidbitting" when they find food. They make soft clucking sounds and pick up and drop the food in a display meant to attract hens. It's part of their courtship behavior.

Playing Dead: Sometimes, when chickens are extremely relaxed or basking in the sun, they can appear as if they are playing dead, lying on their side with their eyes closed and wings slightly spread.

Feather Pecking: This can be a quirky but problematic behavior where chickens peck at each other's feathers. It can be due to boredom, overcrowding, or nutritional deficiencies.

Mimicking Sounds: Chickens are quite adept at mimicking sounds they hear frequently. Some owners report their chickens' making noises that resemble common household sounds or even human speech patterns.

These behaviors contribute to the charm and appeal of keeping chickens, offering endless entertainment and a window into the complex social lives of these fascinating birds.

Setting Up Your Coop

Designing or choosing the right chicken coop is crucial for the health, productivity, and safety of your chickens. A coop provides shelter, protection from predators, and a comfortable environment that can affect your flock's overall well-being.

Chicken Coop Key Design Features

Ventilation: Proper airflow is essential to remove moisture and ammonia, keeping the coop dry and preventing respiratory issues. However, avoid drafts directly on the birds, especially in colder climates.

Space: Chickens need adequate space to move, feed, and roost comfortably. Generally, plan for at least 2-3 square feet per chicken inside the coop and about 10-12 square feet per chicken in an outside run.

Protection: The coop must be secure from predators with sturdy construction, lockable doors, and hardware cloth instead of chicken wire for openings.

Nesting Boxes: Provide one nesting box for every 3-4 hens, placed in a quiet, dark area of the coop for egg-laying. Sized about 14"x14"x14", 1-3 feet off the floor, lower than the roosting bars and add nest box curtains.

Ease of Cleaning: A coop should be easy to clean to maintain hygiene. Consider outdoor access to nesting boxes, features like removable trays, easy access to all areas, and materials that resist pests and rot.

DIY vs. Prebuilt Coops: Building your own coop can be cost-effective and allows for customization to fit your specific needs and preferences. It offers the flexibility to scale the design according to the size of your flock and to incorporate personal touches that enhance the functionality and aesthetics of the coop. A DIY coop may cost as low as $100 to $500 and will require time, tools, and a certain level of skill. Costs can vary but careful planning and sourcing reclaimed materials can keep expenses low.

Prebuilt coops offer convenience and immediate use, with designs ranging from basic to elaborate. They are ideal for those who prefer a turnkey solution without the effort of construction. The downside is that prebuilt coops can be significantly more expensive than DIY options, and the quality varies greatly among manufacturers. Prices for prebuilt coops can range from a $300 - $1000, depending on size, materials, and features.

Essential Equipment: Make sure that your coop contains 1) feeders and waterers which should be accessible, easy to clean, and designed to minimize waste. 2) Roosting bars at different heights with space for all chickens to roost comfortably off the ground and 3) additional lighting during the shorter days to maintain egg production.

Chicken Tractor: A chicken tractor, often part of a mobile chicken coop concept, is a movable structure designed to house chickens while providing them with fresh foraging opportunities. Mounted on wheels, it allows homesteaders to easily relocate the coop across their land. Chicken tractors are an innovative solution for rotational grazing, enhancing soil health and reducing the reliance on chemical fertilizers and pesticides.

Composting Manure: Chicken manure is rich in nitrogen, phosphorus, and potassium, essential nutrients for plant growth. By composting chicken waste, homesteaders can transform it into a valuable organic fertilizer, reducing the need for chemical fertilizers. The composting process neutralizes pathogens and seeds, making it safe for use in the garden. This cycle of waste-to-resource not only enriches the soil but also contributes to a closed-loop system on the homestead.

Integrating Chickens into the Garden: Chickens can play a beneficial role in the garden by naturally controlling pests and aerating the soil. However, chickens will destroy a garden. Chickens like to eat the same types of greens you like to eat and flowers you like to see. And there are predators out there; weasels, hawks and eagles, raccoons and coyote's. It's recommended to keep an eye on your feathery friend when out of the coop.

Living Off-Grid: Homesteading 101

Daily Care & Management:

Proper daily care and management are crucial to maintaining a healthy and productive flock of chickens. This involves consistent feeding, watering, and vigilant health monitoring to ensure your chickens thrive. Here's a look at these essential aspects of chicken care.

Feeding: A balanced diet is essential for the health and productivity of your chickens. The primary diet for most chickens is a commercial poultry feed, which is formulated to provide all the necessary nutrients. Starter feeds are used for chicks under 6 weeks, grower feeds from 6 to 20 weeks, and layer feeds beyond that for egg-laying hens. The specific type of feed will depend on the age and purpose of your chickens (meat vs. egg production).

Food scraps: Supplementing this diet with kitchen scraps, garden waste, and allowing foraging can provide variety and additional nutrients. However, avoid toxic foods like avocado, chocolate, and salty foods.

Grit: Chickens also need grit, small stones or coarse sand, to help digest their food since they lack teeth.

Calcium: Laying hens require extra calcium for eggshell production. This can be provided through oyster shells or eggshell supplements.

Feed and Water Efficiency: Chickens are messy eaters. Minimizing waste in feeding and watering practices is essential. Using feeders that reduce spillage and water systems that keep water clean and reduce evaporation can significantly cut down on waste. Implementing rainwater harvesting systems to collect and store water for chicken use further reduces reliance on external water sources, conserving natural resources.

Watering: Chickens need constant access to clean, fresh water. Dehydration can quickly lead to health issues and decreased egg production. Waterers should be checked and refilled daily, and more frequently during hot weather. To prevent contamination and the spread of disease, clean the waterers regularly, ensuring they are free of droppings and algae.

Winter Care: Chickens are remarkably resilient to cold temperatures. Most chicken breeds can tolerate cold weather especially Plymouth Rock, Wyandotte, and Orpington without the need for additional heating, as long as they are provided with a dry, draft-free coop. Where temperatures reach below 0oF (-18oC) consider using heated waterers to prevent freezing or change the water several times a day to keep it liquid.

Keeping Your Flock Healthy

Regular observation is key to early detection of health issues. A healthy chicken is active, alert, and has a good appetite. A well-balanced diet tailored to the life stage of the chicken supports overall health and immunity, reducing susceptibility to disease. Clean coops prevent the buildup of harmful pathogens and parasites, while adequate space minimizes stress and aggression among birds, further bolstering their health.

Preventative Measures: Maintaining clean living conditions, providing a balanced diet, and minimizing stress will provide for a happy flock. Coop cleanliness is crucial; regular cleaning and disinfecting help prevent disease outbreaks. Providing ample space reduces stress and aggression among chickens, which can lead to pecking and other health issues.

Parasite Control: The presence of external parasites like mites and lice are easily treated with chicken dust baths. This is where a chicken will dig a shallow pit and roll around in the dirt – it's quite effective. Outdoor chickens are very susceptible to worms. Symptoms include a change in behavior, closing their eyes, and eating slows down or stops. Flubenvet is one of the best de-wormers, however there are many brands available that treat all types of worms.

Illnesses: Chickens can fall prey to various illnesses. Signs of illness can include lethargy, reduced egg production, abnormal droppings, coughing, or sneezing. Vaccinations against common diseases like Marek's disease and Newcastle disease are effective preventative measures. Immediate isolation of sick birds, along with prompt veterinary consultation for diagnosis and treatment, is critical in managing health issues. Check with local veterinarians regarding typical vaccinations recommended in your area.

Quarantine New Birds: Introducing new chickens to your flock can introduce diseases. Quarantine new arrivals for at least two weeks to monitor for signs of illness.

Egg Production

Egg production is a key aspect of managing a laying flock, and several factors contribute to maximizing this output, including diet, light management, egg collection practices, and managing broodiness. Typical cost for "Layer" feed is $0.30 - $0.50 per pound and the feed consumption rate should be about 1.75 pounds for 52 weeks would be about $35 - $45.00 per year.

Diet and Nutrition: The diet of laying hens ("Layers") is crucial for high egg production. Layers require a balanced feed rich in protein, calcium, and essential vitamins and minerals. Protein is vital for egg production, while calcium ensures strong eggshells. Layer feed typically contains around 16% to 18% protein and higher levels of calcium compared to feeds for non-laying chickens. Supplementing their diet with oyster shell or crushed eggshell can provide an additional calcium source, essential for those not on a complete layer ration.

Light Management: Light influences the laying cycle of hens. Hens require about 14 to 16 hours of light per day to maintain optimum egg production. As natural daylight decreases in autumn and winter, supplementing with artificial light in the morning hours can help maintain egg production levels. However, it's crucial to gradually increase light exposure to avoid stressing the birds. Sudden changes in light exposure can lead to health issues and decreased egg production.

Egg Collection: Regular egg collection is essential to encourage continued laying and prevent issues like egg eating or breakage. Collect eggs at least once a day, but ideally twice, to keep them clean and reduce the risk of damage. This also helps in identifying any potential problems with the eggs or the health of the hens early on. Store eggs in a cool, dry place before washing and refrigerating.

Managing Broodiness: Broodiness is a natural instinct for hens to sit on and hatch eggs. While this can be desirable in breeding scenarios, it reduces egg production. Broody hens will stop laying, spend their time on the nest, and may become aggressive.

To discourage broodiness: Remove the hen from the nest and place her in a separate coop with good light exposure and no nesting materials. This "broody breaker" coop can help disrupt her broody behavior. Ensure she has access to food and water and monitor her to ensure she returns to normal behavior before reintroducing her to the flock.

Managing a flock for optimum egg production involves understanding and catering to the specific needs of laying hens. A balanced diet, proper light management, regular egg collection, and effective management of broodiness are all key to maximizing the productivity and health of your laying hens. By addressing these areas, you can ensure a steady supply of fresh eggs from your flock.

Raising Chickens for Meat

Raising chickens for meat is a practice that dates back centuries, providing a sustainable source of protein for homesteads and farms. Adhering to regulations and best practices ensures the process is humane, hygienic, and safe.

Best Breeds for Meat Production

When raising chickens for meat, selecting the right breed is crucial for achieving optimal growth rates and meat yield. Broiler chickens, specifically bred for meat production, are the most common choice due to their rapid growth and efficient feed conversion. Popular breeds include:

Cornish Cross: The most widely used meat chicken breed, known for its fast growth, reaching slaughter size in just 6-8 weeks. These birds have a high feed conversion rate and produce a large amount of tender, white meat.

Freedom Rangers: These are a great alternative for those seeking slower-growing breeds that are more suited to free-ranging. They reach slaughter weight in about 9-11 weeks and are known for their flavorful meat.

Heritage Breeds: Breeds like the Jersey Giant and the Orpington take longer to reach slaughter weight (up to 16 weeks or more) but are prized for their richly flavored meat and ability to forage, making them suitable for pasture-raised meat production systems.

Feeding and Growth

Feeding is a critical aspect of raising meat chickens, with diets specifically formulated to support rapid growth and muscle development. Starter feeds are rich in protein to promote early growth, and finisher feeds are adjusted to ensure optimal weight gain towards the end of the growing period. Access to clean, fresh water at all times is essential to support their dietary needs and overall health.

For those raising chickens in a pasture-based system, allowing chickens to forage can supplement their diet with natural sources of nutrition, although this method generally results in slower growth compared to confined feeding strategies.

Humane Slaughter and Equipment Needed

The scope of this book is limited to personal meat consumption. Selling meat to the public may require inspections, permits, or specific processing conditions. For personal consumption, regulations tend to be less stringent but should still be followed to ensure safety and compliance.

Ethical treatment and minimizing stress for the birds throughout the process are paramount, ensuring that the process is as stress-free and painless as possible for the animal. This includes handling the birds calmly, ensuring all equipment is ready before starting, and performing the slaughter quickly and humanely to avoid unnecessary suffering.

Before beginning, familiarize yourself with local regulations regarding home poultry processing. Some areas may require specific sanitary measures or limit the number of birds you can process. Best practices include ensuring a clean, organized workspace; wearing protective clothing; and maintaining sharp tools.

Equipment Preparation: Essential equipment includes:

Killing Cone: Restrains the bird and allows for a cleaner bleed-out.

Sharp Knife: Essential for a quick, clean cut.

Scalding Tank: Heated to the correct temperature (around 140°F to 150°F) to loosen feathers without cooking the skin.

Plucking Machine or Hand Pluckers: Efficiently removes feathers.

Evisceration Table: Clean, sanitized surface for gutting and processing.

Cooling Tank: Filled with ice water to rapidly cool the carcass post-processing.

Packaging Supplies: For storing the meat in the freezer.

Step-by-Step Guide

Preparation: Ensure all equipment is sanitized and ready. Calmly and securely place the chicken in a killing cone or hold it firmly. Make a swift, deep cut across the throat just below the jaw to sever the jugular vein and carotid artery, ensuring a quick and humane death.

Scalding: Once the bleeding stops, scald the chicken by submerging it in the scalding tank for about 30-60 seconds to loosen the feathers. The correct temperature and time are crucial; too hot or too long can cook the skin, while too short or cool makes plucking difficult.

Plucking: Remove the chicken from the scalding tank and proceed to pluck the feathers. Start with the large flight feathers and work down to the smaller body feathers. This can be done manually or with a plucking machine for efficiency.

Eviscerating: Carefully make an incision near the bottom of the bird to remove the entrails, being careful not to rupture the intestines. Gently pull out the intestines, heart, liver (saving the liver and heart if desired), and lungs. Remove the crop from the neck area and the trachea and esophagus.

Cleaning: Thoroughly rinse the bird inside and out with cold water to remove any remaining blood or feathers.

Cooling: Submerge the processed chicken in an ice water bath to rapidly reduce the body temperature, which helps prevent bacterial growth.

Preparing for the Freezer: Once cooled, the chicken can be bagged and labeled for freezing. Ensure all air is expelled from the bag to prevent freezer burn.

References:

The Small-Scale Poultry Flock by Harvey Ussery

Storey's Guide to Raising Chickens by Gail Damerow

Mini-Encyclopedia of Chicken Breeds and Care by Frances Bassom

Beginners Guide to Raising Chickens by Anne Kuo

Relevant Resources:

American Poultry Association – AmerPoultryAssn.com

Backyard Poultry Magazine – BackyardPoultryMag.com

MotherEarthNews.com

Tractor Supply stores.

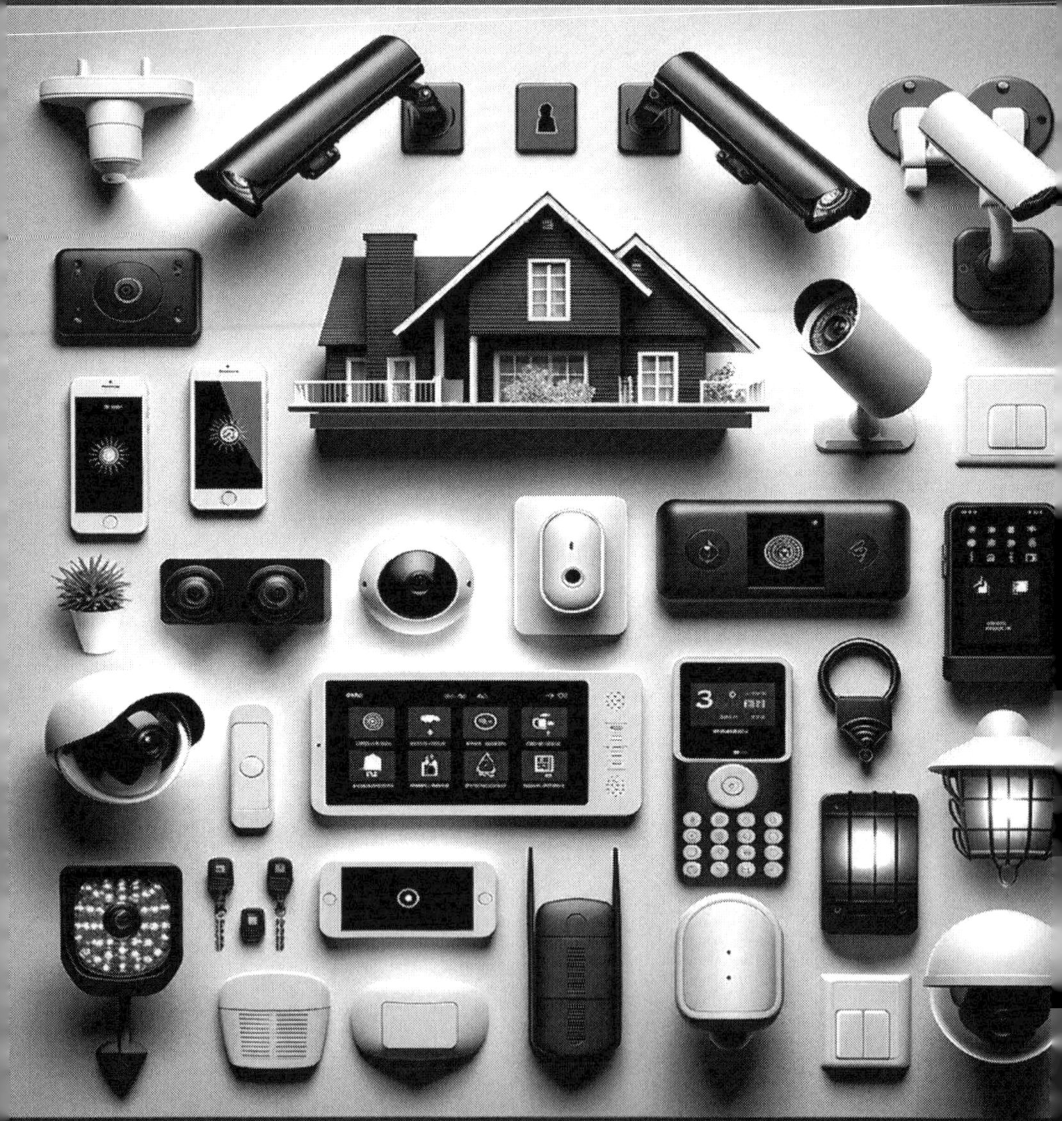

Chapter 10
Ensuring Your Homestead's Security

Picture this: You've invested heart and soul into cultivating a homestead that's both a sanctuary and a bastion of sustainability. But just as a garden requires a fence to protect it from hungry critters, your homestead needs a shield against the less idyllic aspects of rural living. We're not just talking about the occasional lost cow wandering onto your property; we're addressing the real nitty-gritty of security and safety. From weather that can turn-on a dime to wildlife that doesn't know a tomato from a turnip, the threats are real, and so must be your strategies to counter them.

Evaluating Your Homestead's Vulnerabilities

Your homestead is your castle, and like any good fortress, it's only as strong as its weakest point. It's time for a little reconnaissance mission around your domain. Grab a notepad, and let's take a walk—eyes wide open to the potential chinks in the armor.

Every window, door, and even that hole in the fence you've been meaning to fix is a welcome sign to unwelcome guests. Start with the obvious: doors and windows should be sturdy and have secure locks. But don't stop there; consider where a clever raccoon or even a thief could slip through. That overgrown shrub near the window might provide the perfect cover for a break-in, and the tool shed's flimsy lock is an invitation for trouble. It's not paranoia; it's preparedness. Consider the following checklist:

Homestead Vulnerability Checklist

- Check locks on all doors and windows
- Assess the condition of fences and gates
- Inspect outbuildings for security risks
- Evaluate trees, bushes, etc. that may conceal intruders
- Ensure proper lighting around the perimeter

Assessing Natural Disaster Risks

Mother Nature can be a fickle friend. If you're in tornado alley, a storm cellar isn't just a good idea—it's a lifeline. Flood plains, wildfire zones, areas prone to earthquakes—all have unique demands for preparation and fortification. Know the risks inherent to your area and gear up accordingly. Reinforce structures, create defensible spaces against wildfires, and always have an evacuation route planned for quick escape if the forces of nature decide to throw a curveball your way. Ask yourself these questions:

1. Do you know the top three natural disaster risks in your area?
2. Have you reinforced your home's structure against these risks?
3. Is there a clear evacuation route and meeting point for all family members?

Evaluating Local Wildlife Threats

Let's talk critters. Deer are adorable until they destroy your garden. Bears are fascinating unless they're rummaging through your trash. Even smaller wildlife like rabbits or moles can wreak havoc. The idea is to coexist without conflict. This might mean installing higher fences, using wildlife-resistant trash containers, or employing garden layouts that discourage foraging. Think like the animals you're deterring: If you were a hungry critter, what would look tempting, and how would you get to it?

Coexisting with Wildlife Tips

- Use fencing that's appropriate for deterring specific wildlife. Consider height, depth, and material.
- Protect your garden with covers or cages for individual plants or beds.
- Store trash in secure containers, preferably in a locked shed or garage

Ensuring Your Homestead's Security

- Minimize attractants by cleaning up fallen fruit and securing compost bins.

By thoroughly assessing these vulnerabilities, you're creating a blueprint for a secure homestead. It's not about building a fortress; it's about smart, strategic planning that considers every angle—from the ground to the gutters. With your homestead's weak points shored up, you can rest a little easier, knowing you're prepared for the challenges that come with rural living. Remember, it's not just about the defenses you build but also about the peace of mind they provide.

Basic Security Measures for Every Homesteader

In the heart of homesteading, where self-reliance is the creed, the protection of your land and livelihood is paramount. It's not merely about safeguarding against the occasional passerby with a penchant for pilfering; it's about creating a domain that stands vigilant against all manner of intrusion. Here, we delve into the foundational security measures that serve as the bedrock for a fortified homestead.

- **Installing Sturdy Fences and Gates.** A robust fence serves as the first line of defense, a stalwart guardian that delineates your territory and discourages trespassers. Whether you opt for wooden privacy barriers or chain-link enclosures, the goal is clear: to establish a boundary that is both visible and impenetrable. Gates, the sentinels that control entry, should be equally robust and, ideally, outfitted with padlocks or coded locks to control access. In choosing materials, consider the climate and potential threats; a fence that can withstand the local weather and deter local wildlife is a must.

When constructing these barriers, attention to detail can make all the difference. Burying the base deep into the ground can deter burrowing animals, and angling the top outward can dissuade climbers. Regular inspections for damage or wear ensure that your fence continues to stand strong, a silent yet effective shield around the fruits of your hard work.

- **Using Lock Systems for All Entrances.** Your homestead's entrances are more than thresholds; they are potential vulnerabilities that require fortification. Strong, reliable locks are non-negotiable, providing a layer of security that can deter even the most determined intruder. Deadbolts on doors offer a level of protection that standard locksets cannot match, while window locks can prevent stealthy entries.

Consider, too, the convenience of modern technology with keyless entry systems that can track who comes and goes. With features such as personalized codes, you can grant access to family and trusted friends without the risk of lost keys falling into the wrong hands. It's a blend of tradition and innovation, where the age-old lock and key meet the convenience of the digital age.

- **Keeping a Well-Trained Guard Dog.** In the realm of homestead security, a well-trained guard dog is both companion and protector—a loyal ally with an innate sense for detecting threats. The presence of a dog alone can be a powerful deterrent, with their keen senses picking up on disturbances that might elude their human counterparts. The choice of breed is personal, with many opting for those known for their protective instincts, such as German Shepherds, Rottweilers, or Belgian Malinois.

Training is key for these canine defenders to understand their role on the homestead. Obedience training lays the groundwork for discipline, while specialized training can hone their skills for guarding and threat assessment. The bond between a homesteader and their guard dog is one of mutual respect and understanding, with each party playing a vital role in the safety of the homestead.

With each of these measures in place, your homestead stands as a testament to the diligence and care taken to ensure its integrity. Fences and gates mark the perimeter, locks secure the entries, and the faithful guard dog watches over everything. These are the threads that weave the tapestry of a secure homestead, each strand integral to the strength of the whole.

Advanced Security Systems for the Homestead

In the vein of modern homesteading, where tradition meets innovation, we find ourselves looking toward advanced security systems to provide an extra layer of protection. While rustic charm is part and parcel of rural life, there's no reason not to equip your homestead with the latest in security technology.

- **Implementing Surveillance Cameras** A network of surveillance cameras serves as the eyes of your homestead when you can't be everywhere at once. Strategically placed cameras can monitor the comings and goings on your property, providing a visual log that can

Ensuring Your Homestead's Security

be invaluable in the event of an incident. Today's systems offer high definition clarity, night vision capabilities, and even thermal imaging to cut through the thickest fog or blackest night.

Selecting the right cameras for your property is key. Weatherproof models with wide-angle lenses ensure coverage of large expanses of outdoor space, while tilt-and-zoom features allow for close monitoring of sensitive areas. Connectivity is also crucial; wireless systems can transmit footage directly to your smartphone or tablet, giving you the power to survey your domain from anywhere in the world.

- **Installing Motion Sensor Lighting** The sudden illumination of a darkened area is often enough to deter those who would skulk unseen around the edges of your homestead. Motion sensor lighting is a simple yet effective tool in startling would-be intruders and illuminating their activities. These lights, activated by movement within a certain range, cast a bright net over previously shadowed nooks and crannies.

When integrating motion sensor lighting into your security plan, consider the placement of each unit. Aim for coverage of all potential entry points and pathways, as well as areas where shadows may offer concealment. The sensitivity of the sensors can usually be adjusted to avoid false alarms triggered by small animals or rustling leaves, ensuring that the lights activate only when a substantial presence is detected.

- **Using Alarm Systems** An audible alert can serve as a robust deterrent to intrusion and an immediate signal for you to take action. Alarm systems, once the exclusive domain of urban dwellings, have found a place in the countryside, where they offer an additional line of defense. Modern systems integrate seamlessly with cameras and motion sensors, creating a unified network that responds instantaneously to breaches in security.

The siren of an activated alarm is a clear and unambiguous call to attention, one that can not only scare off intruders but also alert neighbors and authorities to potential issues. Many systems also include monitoring services that provide round-the-clock oversight, ready to dispatch assistance at the first sign of trouble. With user-friendly interfaces, these alarms can be set, adjusted, and deactivated with ease, ensuring that they serve as faithful guardians without complicating the simplicity of homestead life.

Incorporating these advanced security measures into your homestead brings a melding of pastoral serenity and modern peace of mind. The cameras, lighting, and alarms stand as silent sentries, blending into the landscape while providing a watchful gaze over your home and hearth. Technology, once thought to be the antithesis of the back-to-the-land ethos, has found its place, offering a discreet yet powerful shield against the uncertainties of the world beyond the farm gate.

Emergency Preparedness

In the heartland of self-sufficiency, where each day unfolds in a symphony of chores and triumphs, the notion of emergency preparedness is not alarmist—it's as fundamental as the morning's first cup of coffee. It's the quiet acknowledgment that sometimes, despite our best efforts, the unexpected can sweep in, urging us to have plans in place not just for the sunny days but also for the storms.

Creating an Emergency Evacuation Plan

When time is of the essence, clarity saves lives. Sketching out an evacuation plan is about drawing a map of the quickest route to safety. It outlines the paths to take when fleeing from danger, be it a wildfire's wrath or a flood's rise. Start by identifying multiple exit routes from your home and property, knowing that one path may be blocked. Assign a meeting point, a safe distance away, where all household members can converge. Rehearse this plan until it's etched in memory, ensuring that when the moment comes, instinct takes over and guides you to safety.

Provisioning for the Long Haul: Essential Supplies

There's a certain art to stockpiling for emergencies. It's a careful curation of goods that ensures survival when modern conveniences falter. Water, non-perishable food, batteries, flashlights, a portable radio—all form the backbone of your emergency kit. But don't overlook the less obvious: copies of important documents, extra clothing, blankets, a first aid kit, prescription medications, and personal hygiene items. These supplies, stored in a readily accessible location, can mean the difference between hardship and relative comfort during times of duress.

First Aid: The Homesteader's Healing Hand

Every homesteader knows the value of a hard day's work—and the scrapes and bruises that come with it. But in an emergency, first aid skills become your most valuable tool. The ability to dress a wound, perform CPR, or set a splint can stabilize a situation until professional help arrives. Take a course, keep a comprehensive first aid manual on hand, and ensure your kit is stocked with more than just band-aids. Your grasp of these skills is a lifeline, a beacon of hope when the lights go out.

Staying Connected: The Communication Lifeline

In today's digital age, we're more connected than ever—but in an emergency, those lines can quickly fray. Establish a communication strategy that doesn't rely solely on cell phones. Designate an out-of-area contact who can relay messages among separated family members. Invest in a hand-crank or solar-powered charger for your devices, consider two-way radios for local communication, and if you're in a remote location, a satellite phone might be a wise addition. Remember, when the grid goes down, your ability to reach out becomes as precious as the food in your pantry.

With these preparations woven into the fabric of your daily life, you stand ready to face the unforeseen with a steadiness that only a homesteader can know. It's the culmination of a lifestyle that values foresight, a testament to your commitment to safeguarding the homestead against all odds.

After all, the true essence of homesteading isn't just about the sunny harvests; it's also about weathering the storms. It's in these moments of trial that the strength of your foundation is tested, and the depth of your resilience is revealed. So you plan, you prepare, and you persevere, knowing that each step taken in preparation today fortifies the future of your homestead.

As the sun dips below the horizon and the stars begin their nightly vigil, take solace in the knowledge that your homestead is not just a place, but a promise—a promise of security, of continuity, and of a steadfast readiness for whatever lies ahead.

References:

The Top 6 Solutions for Rural Home Security System - https://reolink.com/blog/rural-home-security-solutions/

Farm Disaster Preparedness. Considerations in planning for natural disasters on your farm. - https://www.motherearthnews.com/sustainable-living/nature-and-environment/homestead-disaster-preparedness-zbcz2110/

Ways To Treat Wildlife Humanely When Creating A Homestead - https://www.permaculturenews.org/2020/05/04/ways-to-treat-wildlife-humanely-when-creating-a-homestead/

Make a Plan. Create and practice an emergency plan so your family will know what to do in a crisis. - https://www.redcross.org/get-help/how-to-prepare-for-emergencies/make-a-plan.html

Relevant Resources:

Homestead.org

HomesteadersofAmerica.com

Youtube: The Homesteading Guide To Security: Basics by Ravenwood Acres

Ensuring Your Homestead's Security

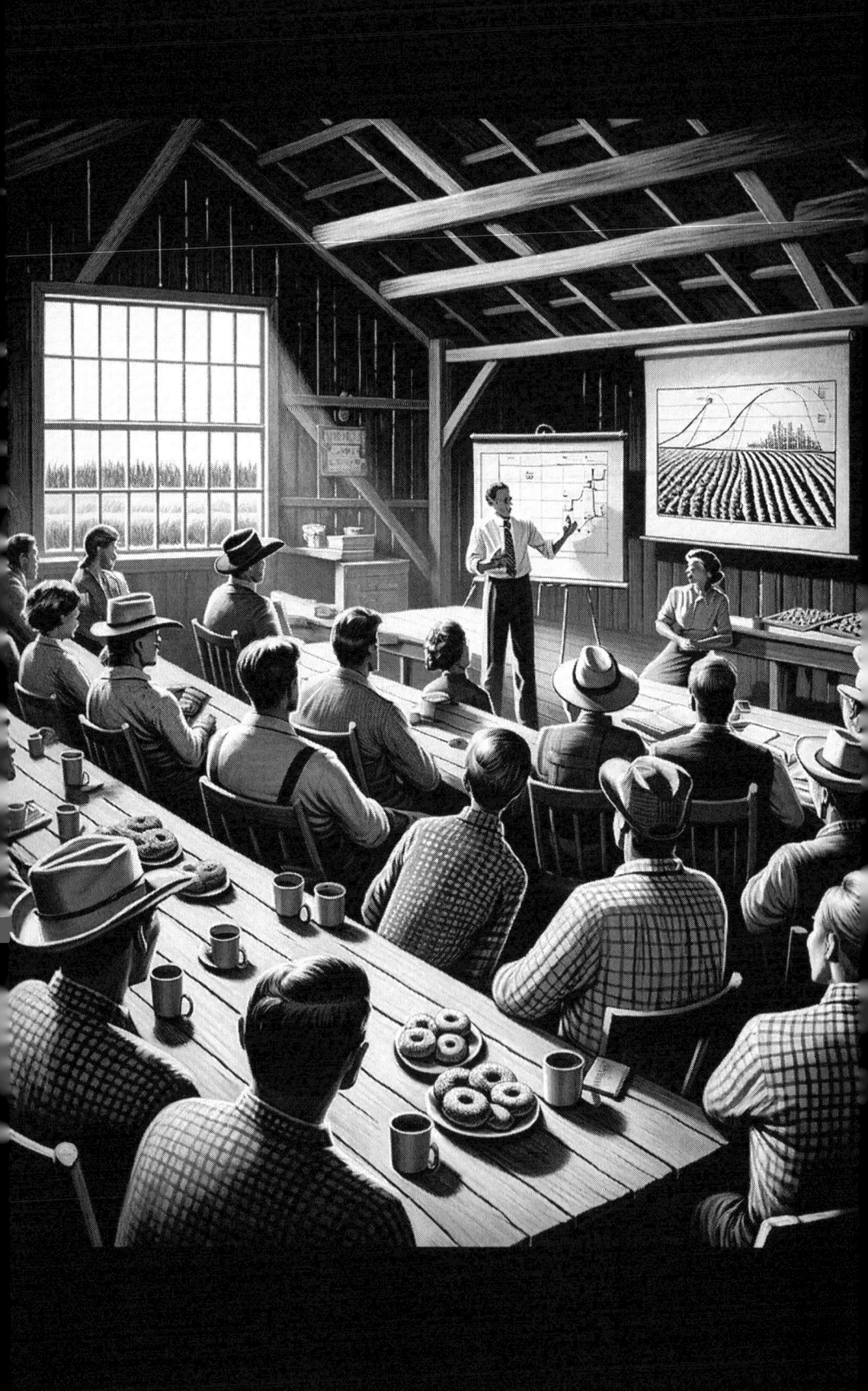

Chapter 11

The Homesteader's Community - Weaving the Social Fabric of Self-Sufficiency

Think of your homestead not as an island but as a vital piece of a larger mosaic, where each tile gains strength and vibrancy from its neighbors. It's easy to picture homesteading as a solitary endeavor, you against the elements, but the truth is far richer. We thrive on connection, on the shared wisdom and collective power of community. This chapter isn't about retreating into solitude; it's about embracing the kind of togetherness that fortifies and enriches our lives as modern homesteaders.

Your entrance into this interconnected world isn't just about trading eggs for milk or borrowing a tiller. It's about laying down roots in a network of mutual support, where the currency is as much about camaraderie as it is about crops. It's the potlucks with laughter floating over the clink of jars filled with your summer harvest, the shared stories over fence lines while trading seeds, and the collective sigh of relief when a neighbor's tractor pulls your truck from a snowdrift. In these moments, the true value of community becomes crystal clear.

The Importance of Community for Homesteaders

Sharing Resources During Scarcity

Times of scarcity can test a homesteader's resolve, but they also unveil the power of community. When drought wilts your fields, it may be a neighbor's well that keeps your garden alive. If hailstorms ravage your apple orchard, a fellow homesteader's surplus can fill the gap in your autumn cider pressing. It's a two-way street where today's giver is tomorrow's receiver, a cycle that weaves resilience into the fabric of local connections.

Learning from Others' Experiences

Every homestead has its own tale of trials and triumphs, each a lesson waiting to be shared. Perhaps your neighbor has battled tomato blight and emerged victorious, or maybe they've perfected a rainwater catchment system that's the envy of the county. Through local gatherings or online forums, tips and tales flow freely, providing a treasure trove of knowledge that's both practical and inspiring. This exchange of experiences is a shortcut to wisdom, saving you from learning everything the hard way.

Providing Emotional Support and Companionship

The homesteading life isn't just about physical labor; it's an emotional journey, too. Having a network of like-minded souls who understand the unique highs and lows can be a lifeline. It's in the shared smiles over a newborn goat or the comforting words during a crop failure that bonds are forged. These connections are the heartbeats of the homesteading community, sustaining us through every season.

Homesteading, in its essence, is about nurturing growth—of crops, of animals, and of relationships. It's in the symbiotic relationships we cultivate with our neighbors that our roots deepen and our homesteads flourish. The power of community lifts us when we stumble and celebrates with us when we succeed. It's the shared laughter, the collective problem-solving, and the common values that stitch us together, creating a tapestry of communal resilience that can weather any storm.

So, as you tend to your land and livestock, remember to also tend to the bonds that connect you to others. They are the invisible threads that strengthen the very substance of your homestead. They are the wellspring of joy, the buffer against hardship, and the shared narrative that tells the story of a life well-lived in harmony with others.

Networking with Nearby Homesteaders

Nurturing connections with fellow homesteaders isn't just about camaraderie; it's a mutual exchange where wisdom, resources, and a helping hand in times of need become part of daily living. These relationships are the bedrock upon which resilient communities are built.

Organizing Regular Community Meetings

Regular local gatherings are the heartbeat of a thriving homesteading community. These get-togethers can be as structured as monthly meetings in the town hall or as casual as coffee mornings on your porch. The key is consistency—having a set time and place where everyone knows they can come together to share stories, swap advice, and discuss community projects. Create a rotating schedule for hosting duties to keep the meetings fresh and inclusive.

Collaborative Decision Making

When neighbors come together, collective decisions on community-wide efforts take shape more organically. Whether it's a communal tool library or a joint response to local issues, these meetings provide a platform where every voice is heard, and action plans are born. Use simple voting methods or consensus-building exercises to ensure decisions reflect the group's collective will.

Workshops and Skill Shares

Regularly scheduled workshops, led by local experts or enthusiastic novices, add layers of knowledge and skill to your community fabric. From canning classes to chainsaw safety, these sessions not only educate but also foster a sense of shared growth and achievement.

Participating in Local Homesteading Events

Local Fairs and Markets

Local fairs and farmers' markets are not merely venues to sell your produce; they're opportunities to showcase the fruits of your labor and to learn from others. Set up a booth, volunteer, or simply attend with an open mind. Observing how others engage with customers or manage their displays can offer valuable insights for your own endeavors.

Homesteading Conferences and Gatherings

Larger-scale conferences and gatherings can serve as a wellspring of inspiration and connection. Here, the exchange of ideas extends beyond the familiar, introducing new techniques and perspectives. Attend these events with an eye for innovation and a willingness to bring back and share what you've learned with your local community.

Supporting Homesteader Businesses

Forge bonds by supporting fellow homesteaders' ventures. Whether it's a bed and breakfast run by your neighbors or a local seed-saving cooperative, your patronage strengthens the community's economic base and demonstrates solidarity.

Setting Up a Community Barter System

A barter system rekindles the age-old practice of trading goods and services without the need for currency. This exchange can be informal, a simple agreement between neighbors, or more organized, with a digital platform or bulletin board where offerings and requests are posted. Determine community needs and encourage a diverse array of goods and services to keep the barter system robust and beneficial for all.

Barter Fairs and Swap Meets

Periodic barter fairs or swap meets can become anticipated events, where homesteaders bring their surplus goods and list the services they offer. These fairs not only facilitate the exchange of items but also become social highlights, where friendships are deepened and the community fabric is strengthened.

Transparency and Value Assessment

In any barter system, transparency in the value assessment of goods and services is crucial. Encourage open discussions about the relative worth of items to ensure fair exchanges. This openness fosters trust and builds a foundation for ongoing reciprocal relationships.

With these strategies in place, you'll find that networking with nearby homesteaders weaves a rich tapestry of interdependence and cooperation. It's in these connections that a community finds its rhythm, its pulse, and its strength.

Engaging with the Wider Community

When you put down roots as a homesteader, your reach often extends far beyond the boundary lines of your property. The wider community beckons—a tapestry of schools, businesses, local governments, and service organizations. Each thread in this tapestry offers unique opportunities for homesteaders to contribute, influence, and educate.

Volunteering for Local Initiatives

Community projects are the "fertile soil" in which the seeds of change and goodwill are sown. Volunteering your time and skills can make a significant impact on both the land and its people. Identify local initiatives that resonate with your homesteading ethos, such as community gardens, park cleanup efforts, or habitat restoration projects.

Community Gardens: Offer your hands and knowledge to help cultivate shared garden spaces. These oases can become outdoor classrooms where you teach composting techniques or demonstrate the principles of permaculture.

Cleanup Efforts: Lead by example and organize groups to clean local parks, rivers, and hiking trails. Show how homesteaders respect and value the natural environment by restoring beauty and function to public spaces.

Habitat Restoration: Partner with conservation groups to restore native habitats. Your understanding of local ecosystems can guide projects that reintroduce indigenous plant species and support local wildlife.

Advocating for Homesteading Practices

In a world where many are disconnected from the sources of their food and the rhythms of the natural world, advocating for homesteading practices becomes an act of stewardship. Engage with policy makers, participate in town meetings, and connect with agricultural extension offices to voice the benefits of self-sufficient living.

Policy Engagement:

Attend council meetings or town halls to discuss the importance of sustainable land use. Advocate for ordinances that support small-scale agriculture, renewable energy, and water conservation.

Educational Outreach

Create informative pamphlets or a blog detailing the ecological and economic advantages of homesteading practices. Distribute them at local events or through social media channels.

Extension Partnerships

Collaborate with agricultural extension programs to bring practical workshops and resources to your community. Your homestead could serve as a model for sustainable practices in action.

Participating in Community Education Programs

Homesteaders possess a wealth of practical knowledge that can empower others to make informed choices about food, energy, and conservation. Participate in or develop education programs that allow you to share this knowledge with the wider community.

Workshops and Seminars:

Teach workshops on organic gardening, rainwater harvesting, or renewable energy installation at local schools or community centers.

School Programs:

Develop partnerships with schools to offer field trips to your homestead or to help create school gardens. Educating the next generation about where their food comes from can plant the seeds for future sustainable practices.

Public Speaking:

Accept invitations to speak at civic groups, libraries, or local clubs. Tailor your talks to the interests of your audience, whether it's a step-by-step guide to starting a vegetable garden or the benefits of reducing household waste.

Your interactions with the wider community serve to weave homesteading into the broader tapestry of society. Through volunteering, advocacy, and education, you become an ambassador for a way of life that honors the earth and fosters independence. This role is not just about sharing what you know; it's about opening doors to dialogue, understanding, and respect for diverse ways of living.

In this interconnected world, your homestead is much more than a plot of land—it's a node in a network of growth, learning, and mutual support. Your engagement with the community plants the seeds of change, nurturing a landscape where sustainability and self-sufficiency are not just ideals, but lived realities.

With each initiative, you help to paint a picture of what's possible when we come together with common purpose and passion. The fruits of these efforts are shared, savored, and sustain the community long after individual projects are complete. Your role in these endeavors is a testament to the spirit of homesteading—a spirit that thrives on collaboration and blooms with the collective efforts of all who call this community home.

Handling Opposition and Skepticism

In any endeavor that steps away from the norm, you're bound to encounter raised eyebrows and tough questions. Homesteading, with its self-sufficient ethos and back-to-basics approach, can sometimes be met with skepticism or outright opposition. Whether it's from local officials who balk at unconventional farming practices or neighbors who just don't "get it," you'll find that patience and clear communication are your best allies in these conversations.

Grounding Discussions in Reality

When faced with doubts, arm yourself with the reality of your daily life. Speak from personal experience about the trials and triumphs of homesteading. This isn't about romanticizing the early morning chicken coop cleanings or sugarcoating the backbreaking work of tilling soil. It's about conveying the authentic experience of self-reliance—the satisfaction of harvesting rainwater for your crops or the pride in producing your own energy from solar panels.

Facts are Friends

Equip yourself with data and research to back up your practices. For instance, when people express concern about the viability of solar energy in your area, have the statistics at hand showing the hours of sunlight your homestead receives and the savings on utility bills you've noted. When conversations turn to organic gardening, be ready with studies that show the long-term benefits to soil health and the ecosystem.

Living Proof of the Benefits

There's no stronger argument for homesteading than the tangible results. Show skeptics the surplus from your garden, the efficiency of your composting system, or the drop in your energy bills. Invite them to taste the difference in a freshly picked tomato from your garden compared to one that's traveled miles to a supermarket shelf. Let the quality of your life and the health of your land speak volumes.

Discovering Common Ground

Sometimes opposition stems from a simple lack of understanding. Take the time to discover what concerns lie at the heart of the skepticism you encounter. Are neighbors worried about property values, or is there a misconception about the appearance of solar panels? Address these concerns directly, finding common ground where your homesteading goals align with their interests. Perhaps it's a shared desire for a cleaner environment or an appreciation for local, quality food.

Patience Wears Down Stone

Resistance to change is a natural human instinct. Remember that patience is a powerful tool. It might take time for others to see the positive impact of your homesteading life. Maintain open lines of communication, and don't be deterred by initial dismissals. The most steadfast skeptic may soften over time, especially as they see your continued commitment and the fruits of your labor.

An Invitation to Dialogue

Keep the conversation going. Invite community members to open house days at your homestead or offer to speak at local events. Sometimes, all it takes

The Homesteader's Community - Weaving the Social Fabric of Self-Sufficiency

is a firsthand look at your sustainable practices in action to turn skepticism into curiosity—or even into genuine interest.

Homesteading is more than a personal choice; it's a statement about the kind of world you want to live in—one where sustainability, self-reliance, and a deep connection to the land are cherished. It's about planting the seeds of this vision in your own backyard and nurturing them, despite the doubts of others.

The journey of a homesteader is one of constant learning, growth, and adaptation. It's an ever-evolving process that blends the wisdom of the past with the innovations of the present to create a sustainable future. It's about sharing this journey with others, even those who may not understand it at first. Through open dialogue, patience, and a steady stream of facts and personal stories, you'll find that even the strongest opposition can be transformed into understanding and respect.

And as the sun sets on another day of tending to the land, you're reminded that the roots you plant aren't just in the soil—they're in the minds and hearts of those around you. As we look ahead, we carry the knowledge that each conversation, each shared experience, and each demonstration of the benefits of this lifestyle brings us closer to a world where homesteading isn't the exception, but a thriving, vital part of the community.

References:

The Importance of Community for Homesteaders - https://www.motherearthnews.com/homesteading-and-livestock/the-importance-of-community-for-homesteaders-zbcz1604/

Build Your Modern Homesteading Community - https://www.motherearthnews.com/homesteading-and-livestock/modern-homesteading-community-zm0z22jjzols/

The Importance of Cultivating Homesteading Community - https://discover.texasrealfood.com/homesteading/the-importance-of-cultivating-homesteading-community

Why millennials are giving up city life to start homesteading - https://www.businessinsider.com/why-millennials-people-are-homesteading-control-uncontrollable-food-feel-safe-2024-1

Relevant Resources:

Homesteaders of America – Podcast

    Homesteaders of America is an organization created by homesteaders, for homesteaders.

Conclusion

Well, my friends, we've traveled quite the path together, haven't we? From the moment we first set our sights on that perfect plot of land, through the trials of constructing a home that sits harmoniously with nature, to generating power from the golden rays of the sun and the whispering winds. Our homesteading journey has been one of transformation—a metamorphosis from eager green thumbs to seasoned stewards of the land, from homesteaders to preppers, ready for whatever Mother Nature or life might toss our way.

Remember those early days? The excitement mixed with a healthy dose of trepidation as we took those first steps towards self-reliance. We've come a long way, learning to capture raindrops like precious pearls from the sky, tucking away our harvest like squirrels preparing for winter, and finding harmony with the land.

And let's not forget the power of adaptation. Just as plants reach for the sun, we, too, must continue to grow—expanding our knowledge, refining our skills, and embracing the ever-changing dance with our environment. As I've learned through my own experiences—from buying and selling homes, to installing solar panels, to witnessing the tangible impacts of climate change—this journey doesn't have a final destination. It's a continuous loop of learning, adapting, and thriving.

I urge you to keep that flame of curiosity alive. Dive into new projects, experiment with different crops, and maybe even try your hand at a new sustainable building technique. Sure, some endeavors might not pan out as hoped, but each one teaches us something valuable, adding another layer to our homesteading know-how.

Conclusion

On a final note, the importance of sustainability and self-sufficiency cannot be overstated. In a world where the unexpected has become the norm, the ability to stand on our own two feet, to provide for ourselves and our loved ones, is not just reassuring; it's empowering. Whether it's the peace of mind that comes with a pantry full of home-canned goods or the quiet pride in generating our own power, these are the threads that weave the fabric of a resilient life.

So, keep your boots muddy, your hands dirty, and your heart in the soil. The homesteading life is one of the most profound statements we can make about the kind of world we choose to live in—one that respects the past, cherishes the present, and sows seeds for a sustainable future.

As we part ways, for now, carry with you the lessons etched into the bark of this journey. Share them with others, nurture them within your community, and let them bloom across your homestead. The world needs more homesteaders, more preppers, more guardians of the good earth—and it starts with you.

Here's to your continued success and the never-ending adventure of homesteading. Now, go out there and keep making a difference, one seed, one raindrop, one solar panel at a time.

Viking Publications of Tennessee

Made in the USA
Monee, IL
08 June 2024